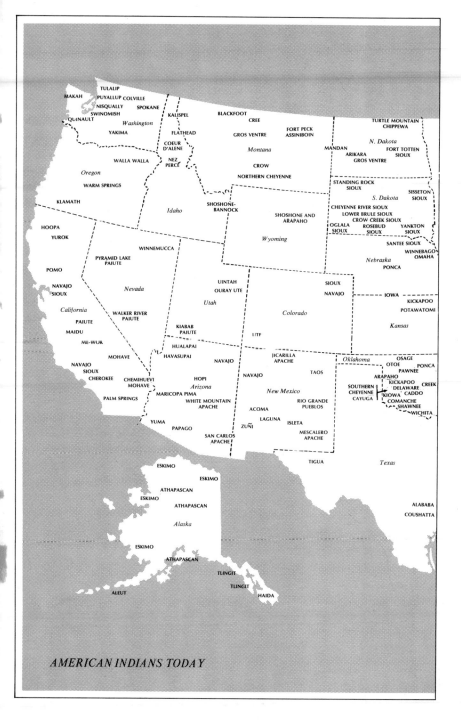

AMERICAN INDIANS TODAY

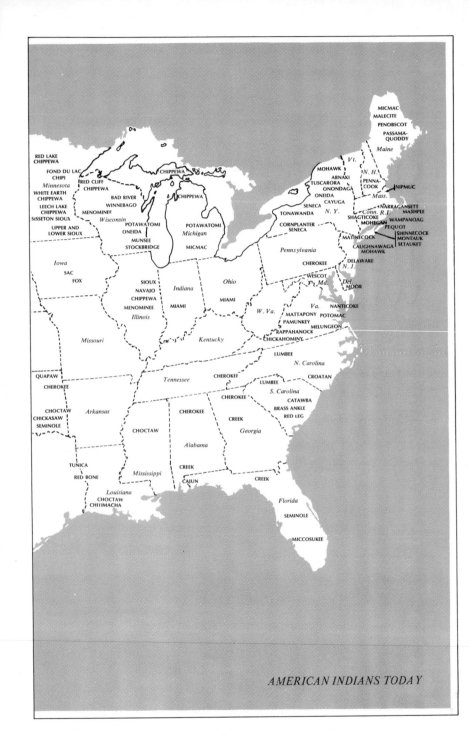

AMERICAN INDIANS TODAY

OUR BROTHER'S KEEPER:
THE INDIAN IN WHITE AMERICA

EDGAR S. CAHN, *Editor*
CITIZENS' ADVOCATE CENTER

A NEW COMMUNITY PRESS BOOK
Distributed by THE WORLD PUBLISHING COMPANY
New York and Cleveland

7

Citizens' Advocate Center

EDITOR: Edgar S. Cahn.
ASSOCIATE EDITORS: Jerry J. Berman, W. Dayton Coles, Jr.,
Nancy Esposito.
RESEARCH: Iris Brest, Sam Deloria, Sylvia Drew, Barbara Dudley,
Clark Gruening, ·Marianne Holifield, Arnold Johnson, Jacqueline
Jones Moore, Joan Nicholson, Francisco Olguin, F. Browning Pipe-
stem, Greg Siggers, Nina Small, Carolyn Smith, Donald Stocks,
Linda Thompson, Tom and Sue Tureen; CONSULTANTS: Jean
Camper Cahn, George Duke, Alvin Josephy, David Littlefield, Peter
MacDonald, Dudley Morris, Joe Muskrat, Gray Orfield, Monroe
Price, Alan Sorkin, Sam Stanley, Vine Deloria, Roger Wolfe;
STAFF: Rosa Colbert, Pat Edgerton, Blanche Gray, Joyce McCoy,
Thelma Neal, Sharon Pipestem, Alzaida Scott, Lulu Stroud, Helen
Taylor; CONTRIBUTORS: Judy Belenky, Katharine Berman, Sergio
Leiseca, Elaine Rapp, Phil Tabas, Alexander Younger.
INDIAN EDITORIAL BOARD: Thomas Banyacya, Mary Cornelius,
Kesley Edmo, Ted Holappa, Johnson Holy Rock, Simon Howard,
Charles H. Lohah, Janet McCloud, Francis McKinley, Cipriano
Manuel, Earl Old Person, Bernard Second, Ernie Stevens.

The *Citizens' Advocate Center* is a non-profit, tax exempt organization designed to monitor governmental programs and assure equitable
treatment of all community organizations in their dealing with the
government. It receives its main financial support from the *Center
for Community Change*. Specific contributions for this book come
from the Field Foundation, Ford Foundation, New York Foundation,
Aaron E. Norman Family Fund and Ruth Thompson.

A New Community Press Book
Published by New Community Press, Inc.
3210 Grace Street, N.W., Washington, D.C. 20007
Distributed by The World Publishing Company
2231 West 110th Street, Cleveland, Ohio 44102
All rights reserved.
Copyright © 1969 New Community Press
Library of Congress Catalog Card Number: 72-97736
Printed in the United States of America
WORLD PUBLISHING
TIMES MIRROR

CONTENTS

FOREWORD

v

PAUL CONKLIN

FOREWORD

Indian. The label is ours, not his. He has been an Indian for only 500 years. For as many as twenty-five *thousand* years, he has been Ottawa, Dakota, Shoshone, Cherokee—or one of several hundred distinct people controlled this continent.

This is a report on the status of these conquered peoples living among us. It is not a scholarly historical analysis of ancient wrongs and promises broken in the distant past. We shrug off history. Rather, it is a look at a world which exists today within our midst—a world hidden from public view and thus from public conscience—a world controlled by white men, a world which grinds out new injustices, new indignities and new wrongs, day by day.

Today the descendants of these original Americans, some 600,000 Indian men, women and children, are the special charges of the Government of the United States.

The world of the Indian is dominated above all by one federal agency, the Bureau of Indian Affairs. He fears, criticizes and attacks this pervasive governmental system ostensibly designed to serve him. Yet, in the absence of any genuine alternative, the Indian vehemently opposes any efforts to dismantle, or even tinker with that system.

The inheritor of defeat, the Indian remains a stranger in his homeland—America's prisoner of war. Despite three centuries of systematic effort to destroy or absorb the American Indian, he shows no sign of disappearing. His culture has been deeply and purposely eroded, yet it persists. His alienation increases, while his numbers grow. The American

Indian, the first American, today is the most invisible of the invisible poor:

—*Indian infant mortality after the first month of life is three times the national average.*

—*The average life span of Indians is 44 years, nearly one-third short of the national average of 64 years.*

—*The Indian's yearly income average, $1,500, is half the national poverty level.*

At first glance the Indian world seems impossibly complex and incomprehensible. Government actions which deeply offend common sense and morality can be, and are, explained away routinely. This complexity is no accident; it is an integral and essential part of a system that relies upon obscurity and intricacy to insulate itself from scrutiny and criticism, and to confound and paralyze both the Indian and the concerned non-Indian.

The numbers involved are small: Indians account for no more than one-half of one per cent of our population. That we have failed with so small a number, however, dramatizes the magnitude of that failure after three centuries of experimentation. We have sought to "Americanize" the most American among us. We have tried to civilize what was considered a handful of uneducated savages and bring them into our Mainstream.

For the past three centuries of social engineering we have failed utterly in many of our goals—failure from which we as a nation would be well advised to learn, lest we repeat our mistakes of a far grander scale with blacks and Mexican-Americans, Puerto Ricans and poor whites.

The Indian bureaucracy—our Brother's Keeper—has now reached a ratio of one official to every 18 Indians. It is, in miniature, the prototype of that great domestic growth industry of our times—the industry charged with the care and tending of the poor. To look at the reservation is to see, in microcosm, the "model neighborhood," the demonstration Appalachian hollow, the pilot migratory labor project. Within this small world of the Indian is to be found the mirror and touchstone of all our national efforts to help others help themselves. In this context, the story of the American Indian becomes a 20th century morality play wherein the Indian assumes the role of Everyman.

This report, then, is a statement about ourselves—about a society so arrogant and insecure that it persists in its efforts to destroy the last vestiges of a culture and people who can serve as a voice of sanity. It is a voice speaking from 25,000 years of experience on this land. We would do well to listen, if we would avoid self-destruction.

—THE CITIZENS' ADVOCATE CENTER
Washington, D.C.
October 1, 1969

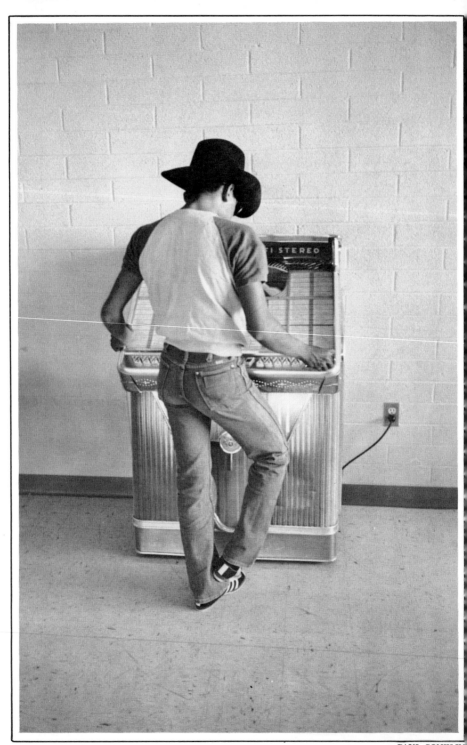

Part One

PIECES OF
A PUZZLE

We began our investigations—not in Washington, and not by reading official reports—but by listening to Indians. On reservations, around ceremonial camp fires, in hogans or houses or huts, on the banks of the Columbia River, in upper state New York, Alaska, New Mexico, California, Oklahoma, the Dakotas, Nevada, the base of the Havasupai canyon—those are the places where we began to listen. The report reflects that perspective—the perspective of those voices we heard—of a composite picture pieced together by a core staff and dozens of researchers, who logged in tens of thousands of miles in the course of the past 10 months.

We do not begin reports with a recitation of isolated achievements—dollars spent, roads paved, sanitary facilities built. For those are dwarfed by an overriding reality that came through countless stories and was subsequently corroborated by extensive analysis of reports, statistics, and studies documenting the extent of poverty, injustice and deprivation.

The report begins where we began—with anecdotes seemingly unrelated, yet all part of a larger picture—with pieces of a puzzle.

On a Chippewa reservation in the Northwest, the children are busily writing a class composition. Their topic is on the blackboard: "Why we are all happy the Pilgrims landed."

At the Pine Ridge Reservation in South Dakota, the second largest in the nation, $8,040 a year is spent per family to help the Oglala Sioux Indians out of poverty. Yet, median income among these Indians is $1,910 per family. At last count there was nearly one bureaucrat for each and every family on the reservation. Over 60 percent of the reservation's work force is without steady employment.[1]

The chief of the Cherokee Indians is picked by the President of the United States—not by the Cherokees. He is W. W. Keeler. He is only fractionally Indian. He cannot even speak to his tribe in its native Cherokee language. But he is Chairman of the Board of Phillips Petroleum Company, an Oklahoma-based oil company that has acquired extensive mineral holdings from Indians in Oklahoma.

Major properties in Palm Springs, California, are owned by the Agua Caliente Indians. To protect these owners from their own improvidence, the Bureau of Indian Affairs permitted state officials to declare nearly two-thirds of them incompetent to manage their own affairs, and to provide guardians or trustees to act for them. It took nine years of complaints to move the BIA to investigate. In 1968 the Secretary of Interior revealed that trustees had been pocketing an average of one-third of the proceeds from the land. In some cases, trustees had been awarded fees as high as 340 per cent of the total receipts.

Haskell Institute, an old Indian college, makes a heavy contribution to the economy of Lawrence, Kansas. At a local restaurant, however, an employee refused to serve the college students. Reminded of the 1964 Civil Rights Act, she responded, "We only have to serve niggers." [2]

Suicides among Indian teen-agers average three times the national rate: on some reservations the suicide rate reaches 10 times the national average. Senator Walter Mondale of Minnesota, describing a visit of Senator Robert F. Kennedy to the Fort Hall, Idaho, Reservation recalls: "We were told that suicides had occurred as early as 10 years of age." Two days after the Indian Education Subcommittee visit, a 16-year-old Indian boy with whom the late Senator Kennedy had chatted committed suicide. He took his life in the county jail, where he had been placed without a hearing and without his parents' knowledge, accused of drinking during school hours. He hanged himself from a pipe extending across the cell. Two other Indians from the same reservation had committed suicide in the same cell, using the same pipe, in the previous 11 months. One was a 17-year-old girl from the same school.

Welfare workers have forcibly removed Indian children from their mothers at Devil's Lake Reservation, North Dakota, placing them with white families. One observer said Indian children run and hide at the approach of unfamiliar cars, and Indian adults reportedly are afraid to speak out for fear they will lose their children. Families claim they have been removed from welfare rolls to force them to surrender their childen for placement off the reservation.

In the State of Washington, Indians who once were prosperous now go hungry because the State will not allow them to fish. The State of Washington spends up to $2,000 per salmon to protect these fish for sportsmen and commercial fisheries, which catch over 90 per cent of the salmon. But it refuses to permit the Indians, who catch less than 10 per cent of the salmon, to continue to fish. The right to fish forever was promised to the Indians by the United States Government in exchange for taking away Indians' land.

An Indian child in the State of Washington objected to the American history text that called her ancestors "dirty savages." The girl was then summarily expelled from the public school there. The reason: the child was "uncontrollable." The mother was forced to send her daughter all the way to Oklahoma to the Bureau-run Fort Sill, Oklahoma, Boarding School. Hundreds of other "uncontrollable" and "problem children" are routinely shipped thousands of miles

from home—some from Alaska to Oklahoma—to BIA board-
ing schools. They see their parents once a year, if that often.

In New Mexico, the Taos Pueblo Indans are fighting
for their holy land, the Blue Lake area in the northern part
of the State. They want it kept free from desecration by
lumber companies and tourists. The legal and moral validity
of their claims to the land has been upheld repeatedly by
federal courts and the Interior Department. Still, Congress
seeks to open the land to tourism and exploitation. The
Indians have been required to "prove" that the land is holy,
and that they use each inch of it, continuously, for their
religious ceremonies.

Indians in California are reluctant to take part in federal poverty programs for fear they later will be billed for
the cost of the programs. Their fear is justified. Over the
past two decades they have been repeatedly charged for
federal expenditures in California relating to Indians during
the 19th century. The charges are deducted from money
owed to the Indians for land seized by the Government. In
many instances, the goods provided to Indians were shoddy.
In some cases they never were delivered. To this day, the
California Indian Legal Services Program financed by the
Office of Economic Opportunity has been unable to secure a
guarantee from the Government that legal services which
it provides to Indians will not be billed to them in the future.

The more the story varies, the more it remains the
same—and slowly, a coherent picture emerges.

THE INDIAN AND HIS KEEPERS: INSIDE A CLOSED WORLD

The Indian is never alone. The life he leads is not his to control. That is not permitted. Every aspect of his being is affected and defined by his relationship to the Federal Government—and primarily to one agency of the Federal Government: the Bureau of Indian Affairs.

From birth to death his home, his land, his reservation, his schools, his jobs, the stores where he shops, the tribal council that governs him, the opportunities available to him, the way in which he spends his money, disposes of his property, and even the way in which he provides for his heirs after death—are all determined by the Bureau of Indian Affairs acting as the agent of the United States Government.

The Bureau of Indian Affairs came into being symbolically and functionally as a division of the War Department in 1834. The Bureau defined Indians as sovereign nations with whom one entered into peace treaties and enforced promises to cease hostilities.

In time, treaties came to be unnecessary. The Indian could simply be regulated and ruled by act of Congress as a subject people. In 1849 the Bureau of Indian Affairs was transferred from the War Department to the Department of the Interior, where it remains to this day. Since then, the Indian has been defined in terms of the land areas reserved for a conquered people. The Bureau's relationship to the Indian became defined in terms of the administration of Indian land, the discharge of treaty obligations respecting that land, and the implementation of those duties owed a conquered and subject people. The Bureau became the army of occupation exercising all powers necessary to govern the conquered Indian territories. Certain of those powers remain to this day. Laws on the books give the Federal Government and the Bureau authority to abrogate treaties with any tribe with whom the United States is at war; prevent the introduction of all goods into Indian country, in the public interest; prohibit the issuance of food rations to the head of any Indian family with children between the ages of eight and 21 who do not attend school; and to authorize the use of vacant army posts and barracks for Indian schools.

And then in 1924, came a new definition: Indians were granted citizenship. The Bureau's responsibilities were broadened to include both the discharge of previous treaty obligations, and the administration of programs created by Congress to give the "new citizen" proper training.

The granting of citizenship to Indians expanded, rather than limited, the BIA's control. New resources were put at the Bureau's disposal, and new programs guaranteed further extension of the Bureau's reach into every aspect of the Indians' individual and communal lives. The Bureau must then be comprehended as a system permeating every dimension of Indian life and every element of Indian activity. More than just the sum of its parts or an aggregate of responsibilities, the relationships between the Indians and the Bureau of Indian Affairs together comprise a total and separate world.

As trustee, governor and benefactor of the Indian, the Bureau of Indian Affairs is a pervasive presence in the Indian world. The Indian's life can be measured in encounters with his Keepers as they make their appointed rounds. The BIA domain touches most states and covers more than 50 million acres which belong to the Indians. The BIA effectively governs the 400,000 Indians on the reservations, and heavily influences the lives of 200,000 living elsewhere. At the huge and fort-like Pine Ridge, South Dakota reservation, an observer likened the Bureau's presence to the British occupation of equatorial Africa.

"The Bureau of Indian Affairs is *the* economic and political force. . . . Bureau personnel attend most public meetings and usually call them to get the Sioux to agree to some program or other, and direct them as well. The school teachers are federal employees in the Bureau. The local Indian who drives the school bus is a Bureau employee. The social worker who calls at an Indian home is part of the same federal bureaucracy. Tribal projects are supervised by Bureau officials. . . .

"After living on the Pine Ridge Reservation for a few months, one cannot help falling into the habit of looking back over one's shoulder now and then," the observer concluded.[1]

The Bureau, unique among federal agencies, is the federal, state and local government of the Indians, and supplants or dominates the private sector as well. It is realtor, banker, teacher, social worker; it runs the employment service, vocational and job training program, contract office, chamber of commerce, highway authority, housing agency, police department, conservation service, water works, power company, telephone company, planning office; it is land developer, patron of the arts, ambassador from and to the outside world, and also guardian, protector and spokesman. Based in Washington, D.C., the Bureau's 16,000 employees are located in outposts extending like tentacles westward from the Potomac.

The BIA Commissioner has his own "cabinet" in Washington—six departments or branches, each with a staff: Community Services, Economic Development, Education, Administration, Engineering and Program Coordination. This structure is duplicated on a regional level in Area Offices, headed by Area Directors. It is duplicated a third, and even a fourth, time at the reservation—or agency and sub-agency —level. Behind every official looking over every Indian's shoulder, there are several layers of officials looking over each others' shoulders.

The authority of the Bureau in every realm of Indian life is absolute both as a legal and practical matter. A Harvard Law Review article summed it up:

"Although the normal expectation in American society

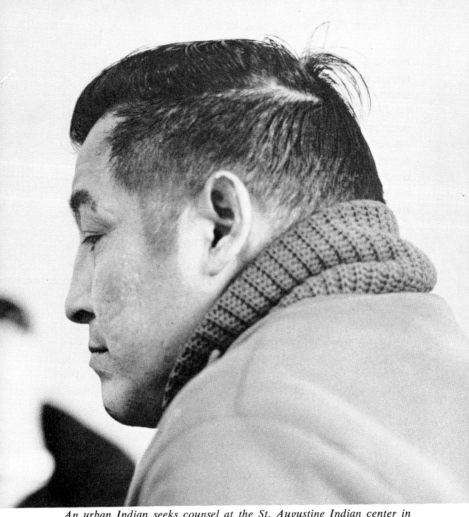

An urban Indian seeks counsel at the St. Augustine Indian center in Chicago.   ED ECKSTEIN

is that a private individual or group may do anything unless it is specifically prohibited by the Government, it might be said that the normal expectation on the reservation is that the Indians may not do anything unless it is specifically permitted by the Government." [2]

The BIA defines who is an Indian. It defines tribes, and can consolidate tribes at will. The Shoshone and Bannock peoples, for instance, have been forced to live together at

Fort Hall Reservation, Iowa, and deal with the Bureau as one tribe. The Bureau decides how tribal membership is determined and supervises admission to tribal rolls.

Nowhere is the BIA's authority better demonstrated than in its power over tribal and individual Indian trust property. The use of Indian land is controlled by the Bureau, as are sales, exchanges and other land transactions. The Bureau prescribes the number of cattle which may graze on a parcel of land. It approves leases, controls prices, terms and conditions. Often the leasing process is initiated not by the owner of the land, but by the person desiring to lease it. Leases have been approved without the owner's consent and *only* the Bureau—not the tribe or individual owner—is empowered to cancel a lease. Under certain circumstances the Bureau can sell timber on Indian land without the owners' consent, and get grant rights of way and permission to build roads, pipelines and even dams.[3]

Even the Indian's personal property is controlled by the Bureau. The Indian may be an adult—and perfectly sound in mind and body. But he still can be treated by the Bureau as legally incompetent to manage his own affairs.

Mere supposition by a Bureau official that an Indian might prove indiscreet in handling money, might be exploited, or might at some future point be unable to provide for himself—any of these is considered reason enough to relieve the Indian of control over his possessions. Once the Indian is deemed incompetent he cannot even draw money from his own bank account without obtaining approval from a BIA guardian. The decision is virtually unchallengeable.

The Indian can, however, count on being treated as "competent" for at least one purpose—to sell his land. He may not be competent to lease it or to mortgage it, but if he needs money he will find the BIA most willing to help sell his land. When an Indian is hungry and desires welfare assistance, the Bureau may devise an acceptable pretext for authorizing the sale or may simply declare his land—land held in trust for him and his heirs forever—an "available asset" which he must utilize before qualifying for welfare.

Once he has sold the land, the Bureau insists that the Indian spend the money from it before qualifying for welfare—but with restrictions. The money becomes subject to BIA control; it is doled out to the Indian at the welfare rate, which is usually below subsistence level.

In its own fashion, the Bureau looks after the education of its younger wards. The BIA operates boarding schools for some Indians, and contracts with local schools for the rest. But what lawyers call *in loco parentis*—"parents by proxy"—has disturbing implications when children are taken from their parents and transported as far as 6,000 miles from Alaska to Oklahoma boarding schools. The Bureau decides where Indian schools will be built and who will attend them. In the case of a Bureau school in Oregon, no Oregon Indian children or Indian children from the Northwest are permitted to attend. The Bureau can close a school and dispose of it without consent of the tribe it serves whenever it is judged that "the good of the service will be promoted thereby." [4]

Tribes must secure the consent of the Bureau to meet and discuss their constitutions. The Bureau decides whether a tribe's chosen form of government is acceptable, and nearly all tribal government decisions must be reviewed by BIA officials.

Even when exercised illegally, the total power of the Bureau is virtually unchallengable and unreviewable. Where the normal citizen has three avenues of redress—political, judicial, administrative—the Indian has none.

Politically he is impotent. He lacks significant voting power. Even where there are sufficient concentrations of Indians to have some impact they are frequently disenfranchised. Every politician loves to pose with Indians, but very few feel compelled to listen to them.

The Indian has no effective administrative remedy. The Indian Affairs Manual, which explains and sets forth the procedures and rules that govern Indians, fills 33 volumes which stack some six feet high. And this manual is not available to the Indian—except at some BIA office, if they choose to let him glance at it. There are more than 2,000 regulations, 389 treaties, 5,000 statutes, 2,000 federal court decisions and 500 opinions of the Attorney General which state, interpret, apply or clarify some aspect of Indian law. Even the Bureau is confounded by its rules. In 1957 the BIA Commissioner wrote: "The uncertainty of our position and the generally adamant, but in the main equally uncertain, knowledge on the part of Indian people concerning their 'treaty rights' make it necessary that such 'rights' be clarified without further delay to facilitate program planning with individual groups." That day of clarification has not come.

The Bureau has a difficult time following its own rules and regulations. Nothing has changed since 1961 when the Task Force on Indian Affairs, in its report to the Secretary of the Interior, criticized "the slow rate at which the Bureau performs its abundant paperwork. Items initiated in the field often must move through a network of reviews and appeals all the way to the Secretary's office, with numerous side trips to specialists and solicitors."

The frustration of this jungle of rules and writ is magnified for the Indian, because normally he cannot obtain a lawyer to help him understand them. Despite a federal law which requires that Indians be provided with legal representation by the U.S. Attorney, very few are in fact provided. Further, no tribe can hire a lawyer without the approval of the Federal Government.

The Bill of Rights was extended to Indians in 1968, but even so, hired lawyers representing Indians at times have been barred from a reservation. For the overwhelming majority of Indians there are still no lawyers available, and without lawyers, rights are just cruel, unfulfilled promises. Even the courts, the forum of last resort and the ultimate source of protection against injustice, become, as a practical matter, unavailable to Indians.

The BIA's plenary and unreviewable power to govern, to assist and to fulfill solemn promises has a tremendous potential for good, but it has equal potential for harm. In practice, the exercise of this power has been used primarily to frustrate the purposes for which it was intended: the social, political and economic self-realization of the Indian.

The failure to accomplish the goals sought for the Indians stems from a perversion of the Federal Government's relationship with the Indian. All Bureau responsibilities and powers stem from its unique obligation to stand as trustee for the nation to honor and implement promises to the Indians.

Other people besides Indians have trustees; other persons besides Bureau officials have fiduciary obligations. Such relationships exist between banker and depositor, lawyer and client, doctor and patient. That relationship does not normally imply any stigma of inferiority or incompetence. But in discharging its trustee responsibilities, the Bureau has perverted its ties to the Indian to a most narrow relationship —that of a competent to an incompetent, a parent to a child, a guardian and his ward.

Felix Cohen, one of the nation's experts on Indian law, noted that in the white man's business world a trustee has no control over his beneficiary's person, but merely attends to the interests of his properties. "In the Indian's world, the same principles should apply; there is no legal basis for the common view that the Indian Bureau may deal with Indian trust property as if it were the owner thereof, or use such power over lands and funds to control Indian lives and thoughts. . . .

"Over the years, any order or command or sale or lease for which no justification could be found in any treaty or act of Congress came to be justified by BIA officials as an act of 'guardianship,' and every denial of civil, political, or economic rights to Indians came to be blamed on their alleged 'wardship.' Under the reign of these magic words nothing Indian was safe. The Indian's hair was cut, his dances were forbidden, his oil lands, timber lands, and grazing lands were disposed of, by Indian agents and Indian commissioners for whom the magic word 'wardship' always made up for any lack of statutory authority."

Constant use of that concept has given it permanence and acceptance in public opinion, but as Cohen notes, "it remains an illusion, unsupported by legal authority." [5]

Through the pervasiveness of the Bureau's role, the exercise of power and administration of programs by the BIA have come to ensure that every effort by the Indian to achieve self-realization is frustrated and penalized; that the Indian is kept in a state of permanent dependency as his price of survival; and that alienation from his people and past is rewarded and encouraged for the Indian.

But somehow, the Indian persists in defining himself— as a man, a divinely created being:

> *"The gods and the spirits of the Sacred Mountains created Man. He was made of all rains, springs, rivers, ponds, black clouds, and sky. His feet are made of earth and his legs of lightning. White shell forms his knees, and his body is white and yellow corn; his flesh is of daybreak, his hair darkness; his eyes are of the sun. White corn forms his teeth, black corn his eyebrows, and red coral beads his nose. His tears are of rain, his tongue of straight lightning, and his voice of thunder. His heart is obsidian; the little whirlwind keeps his nerves in motion, and his movement is the air. The name of this new kind of being was 'Created from Everything.' "* [6]

THE BUREAU OF INDIAN AFFAIRS:
THE LESSER OF TWO EVILS

The Indian tolerates his present impotent and unjust status in his relations with the Federal Government because he sees the Bureau of Indian Affairs as the lesser of two evils. The BIA is all he has, and every promise to replace it with something better has been broken.

Those new to Indian problems and enraged by the conduct of the BIA, and even those long acquainted with the Bureau's impenetrable bureaucracy often reach an obvious conclusion: why not just do away with the Bureau and, in the words of a U.S. Senator, "free" the Indian?

The easy answer is the wrong answer, and the Indian knows it better than anyone else. Those who would abolish the Bureau to "help" the Indian will find as their most vehement opponent the Indian himself. He knows that he must, even at the cost of his liberty, preserve the Bureau— because the Bureau and only the Bureau stands between the Indian and extinction as a racial and cultural entity. Only the Bureau stands between the Indian and total, unilateral renunciation of all federal treaty obligations. The Bureau has been and only the Bureau remains the special protector of the Indian and his champion, at times, against predatory interests. The Bureau and the solemn promises of the Federal Government are symbolically synonomous in the mind of the Indian. To destroy one is to destroy both.

The Bureau has done a terrible job; it has compromised the Indian time and again; it has permitted, tolerated, even assisted in the erosion of Indian rights and the whittling away of the Indian land base. Still, to the Indian, it is *his*.

In the light of wisdom gained from long years of bitter experience, the Indian knows that a threat to the Bureau, an attack on the Bureau or any change in its structure is to be resisted as a threat to his own survival. Thus, in April, 1969, newspapers around the nation carried stories of atrocities, brutality, mismanagement and professional incompetence at the Chilocco Indian School in Oklahoma. The accounts were based on disclosure of a report by BIA staff investigators.

Yet, a few days later, the newspapers told of rallies by Chilocco students to defend it against these attacks and "save our schools." Were the rallies instigated by Bureau school officials? Perhaps, in part. The fact is, however, that Indian students at Chilocco know despite alleged abuse and its faults, the school is preferable to the total isolation, the prejudice, the humiliation, and the degrading condescension which they meet in public schools. Standards may be low and conditions almost intolerable, but students and graduates at Chilocco at least are permitted to retain an Indian identity. Because of that identity, they develop a solidarity and a sentimental attachment to a school which at least shields them partially from the cultural assault they experience elsewhere.

Similarly, those who try to make changes in the Bureau will find themselves met with substantial opposition from Indians. Thus, a proposal in 1964 to shift the education functions of the Bureau over to the Office of Education in the Department of Health Education, and Welfare was resisted violently by Indians who saw it as a first step toward dismantling the Bureau, abrogating federal responsibilities and turning over Indian education to state education agencies.

The much heralded Omnibus Bill of 1967 which provided, among other things, sorely needed capital funds for economic development and land consolidation, was defeated in part because the Indians perceived it as an attempt to facilitate the withering away of federal obligations.

A proposal adopted in May 1969 by the National Congress of American Indians to streamline the Bureau by abolishing the middle tier of unresponsive bureaucracy, was coupled with an expression of fear: "If the Bureau of Indian Affairs is abolished or its services fragmented, it will again jeopardize, and in many cases it will terminate the present services of the Federal Government. It will be termination in disguise."

Indians can and often do criticize the Bureau, but they do not necessarily regard the non-Indian critic as an ally. They know that criticism can play directly into the hands of their worst enemies—those who wish to end the special relationship which exists between the Indian and the Federal Government.

Even the truth is to be resisted, if it is a truth which can endanger their protector, the Bureau. The Bureau plays upon this fear to stimulate Indians, and particularly tribal leaders, to attack and deny any report which seeks to tell the truth—although the same Indians privately will admit the truth of the charges, and even cite examples.

The Indian not only tolerates the injustice of the system; he helps insulate it from scrutiny and criticism, because history has convinced him that an attack on the Bureau will lead to the destruction of his special status as an Indian, and to the death of his people. This fear takes a particular form—fear of "Termination."

TERMINATION—An end to the special status of the Indian, and with it a disavowal of his trusteeship and protection arrangement with the United States Government. Fear of termination pervades Indian thinking. It colors the Indian's appraisal of every proposal, suggestion and criticism.

Termination refers to that policy officially adopted by the Federal Government in the 1950's, "freeing" the Indian from the BIA's paternalism. But to the Indian, termination is just the latest and most deadly in a series of policies of destruction which has prevailed for nearly two centuries. Earl Old Person, a leader of the Blackfeet Tribe, points out:

> ". . . (I)n our Indian language the only translation for termination is 'to wipe out' or 'to kill off.' We have no Indian words for termination. . . ."

The threat of termination remains strong and reduces the Indian's limited options still further.

". . . (H)ow can we plan our future when the Indian Bureau constantly threatens to wipe us out as a race? It is like trying to cook a meal in your tepee when someone is standing outside trying to burn the tepee down. . . .

"In the past 190 years, the U.S. Government has tried every possible way to get rid of the troublesome Indian problem. . . . First the Government tried extinction through destruction—where money was paid for the scalps of every dead Indian. Then the Government tried mass relocation and containment through concentration —the moving of entire tribes or parts of tribes to isolated parts of the country where they were herded like animals and fed like animals for the most part. Then the Government tried assimilation—where reservations were broken up into allotments (an ownership system the Indians did not understand) and Indians were forced to try to live like 'white men.' Indian dances and Indian hand work was forbidden. A family's ration of food was cut off if anyone in the family was caught singing Indian songs or doing Indian hand craft. Children were physically beaten if they were caught speaking Indian languages. Then termination was tried by issuing forced patents in fee [fee simple title] to Indian landowners—land was taken out of the trust relationship with the U.S. Government and an unrestricted patent in fee was issued to the Indian whether he wanted it or not or whether he understood what was going on or not." [1]

The Indian was correct in his appraisal of termination as annihilation rather than emancipation. Events of the past decade have more than confirmed his worst fears. The Menominee Tribe of Wisconsin, terminated in 1961, symbolizes the nightmare come true. Members of the tribe were proud and relatively self-sufficient people with good schools, community services and a tribal-owned sawmill. Once terminated, their reservation became incorporated into a county, and today it is the most impoverished county in the state. State Public Assistance costs in Menominee County soared from

$121,686 in 1961 to $766,601 in 1968. Menominee County ranks at or near the bottom of Wisconsin's Counties in income, housing, property value, education, employment, sanitation, and health. The median income for the Menominee is below $1,000. Much Indian land has been sold at auctions because Indians were unable to pay the state property taxes to which their land became subject after termination.[2]

The State of Wisconsin has neither the money nor the inclination to assume the responsibilities abandoned by the BIA. The tribal sawmill, inefficient and outmoded, could not provide enough jobs. The county tax base is too small to support decent schools and health services. The Menominee hospital, one of the best for Indians, was forced to close. Indians even lost the right to hunt and fish on their own lands without paying for a state permit—until the Supreme Court decided that the Menominee still hold that right because Congress had "forgotten" to abolish it.

In February 1965, 11 years after termination, a BIA report to Congress gave an accurate portrayal of the effects of termination: ". . . The impact of developments since 1961 on the people of the county cannot be simply characterized. Some Menominees seem to be as demoralized as any poverty-stricken people anywhere. Others, far from demoralized, are highly and vocally indignant."

Professor Gary Orfield, in a study of the tribe conducted at the University of Chicago, commented: "Freedom was the fundamental objective. . . . The failure to extend the real freedom of the tribe has been almost total. . . . The Menominee tribe is dead, but for no good reason."[3]

The Klamath Indians of Oregon fared no better after their emancipation from BIA paternalism. Senator Ralph W. Yarborough of Texas gave this summary: "Their reservation was terminated . . . the lands sold and money distributed. And now . . . somewhat less than 10 years later, the number who finished high school is very small compared to the number who finished high school when they had the reservation. Suicides have increased—this is among the adults—at a terrific rate, drunkenness at a terrific rate, and criminal records are a serious problem." [4]

Similar results from forced termination can be found among the Utah Paiutes. In no case can it be shown that a tribe gained in self-sufficiency after termination: most ceased to exist as cohesive communities with their own culture and history. Even today there is unrelenting pressure to terminate the Colville Indians in Washington state, and in California members of the Agua Caliente Bands are being pressured unscrupulously to abandon the trust status of their land.

Indians were not given any choice about the termination policy of the 1950's. During this period, BIA commissioners were appointed who supported the idea of ending federal-Indian relations. One was Dillon Myer, who gained his government experience as the head of the War Relocation Authority, the agency which directed the internment of the Japanese in the Western U.S. during World War II.

Typically, termination has been forced down the throats of the Indians—by unilateral dictation, deception, and fraud. An assistant commissioner explained, "We did not feel that it was necessary for us to go back to the tribe . . . and start trying to draft a new program. . . ."[5] Fear of termination and continuing intense Congressional pressure for it forces Indians to defend the very agency which wrongs them. This fear paralyzes the Indian and mutes his efforts to change his way of life.

Although termination has been officially discarded as federal policy by the Kennedy, Johnson and Nixon Administrations, the Indian has sound reason to believe that termination lies behind each new reform which the Government poses for Indians. He need only examine the statements at a 1967 Senate hearing of Robert Bennett, the first Indian Commissioner of the BIA in this century and a supposed champion against termination, to see how rhetoric changes, but the underlying purposes persist:

SENATOR HATFIELD: ". . . What is the basic philosophy of the Bureau of Indian Affairs at this time?"

MR. BENNETT: ". . . The basic philosophy is that the Government has made commitments to the Indian people . . . and the Government should carry out these commitments. . . . When the Government has carried out these commitments . . . in the way of their educational level, health level and so forth, then I feel, as Commissioner of Indian Affairs, I have a responsibility to report this to the Congress, and that the Congress, as the policymaking body, will then determine whether or not our services shall be withdrawn and terminated or whether for reasons that the Congress may decide they shall be continued. . . ."

SENATOR HATFIELD: "In other words, termination is the basic philosophy that we are moving toward as each group is brought to a place where they are considered to be self-supporting and self-sufficient; is that correct?"

MR. BENNETT: "Yes, sir. Then the tribal leaders have said when Congress gets through and has carried out their commitments, then they will all have to face this question." [6]

The Indian knows that termination takes many forms. He can be flooded out of his reservation; he can be relocated; his reservation can be sold out from under him if he cannot meet taxes to which it is subject. His limited power to protect himself on the reservation from local prejudice and discrimination can be wiped away by the substitution of state laws for tribal law, and state jurisdiction for tribal jurisdiction. All of these, the Indian knows, are variants on one basic truth: the United States Government does not keep its promises. Sometimes it breaks them all at once, and sometimes slowly, one at a time. The result is the same—termination. When the Indian is asked to forsake his status under the Bureau in exchange for cash, for promises of technical aid, for public works improvements and industrial developments, he has learned to expect two things:

 —*That the promises will not be kept.*

 —*That even if they should be kept, they will prove inadequate to maintain the Indian at even his reservation level of deprivation.*

Rosebud Sioux living in tent on reservation.

As Wendell Chino, President of the National Congress of American Indians, stated, "We American Indians are tired of proposals which offer limited assistance and exact, as the price, the risk of losing our traditional protections afforded by our federal trusteeship." [7] The Indian has learned that he is better off with the Bureau than with the substitutes which have been offered in the past.

A 1969 White House report on Indian problems noted,

"The termination issue still 'poisons' Indian affairs and causes almost every proposal and act of government in the field of Indian affairs to be viewed by the Indians, first, with suspicion and a genuine concern for possible termination motives or results." [8]

For all these reasons, any report which is critical of the BIA places the Indians in a difficult spot. Criticism, even when valid, can backfire. Criticism can be misused to increase the pressure for eliminating the BIA, and with it the special obligations of the nation to the Indians. Criticism can bring termination, and termination in any of its forms is evil. It has wrought only havoc, misery, increased deprivation, and total destruction. Termination, in all of its forms, has been a way to break promises, not fulfill them.

Until reform and termination are separated in the reformer's schemes as well as in the Indian mind, the Indian will continue to defend his Keeper. In that world, the Indian suffers a slow death, but he still can cling to hope. That is the lesser of two evils.

Part Two

HOW NOT TO HELP A PEOPLE HELP THEMSELVES; A SELECTIVE EXAMINATION OF GOVERNMENTAL APPROACHES TO THE INDIANS

We turn now from a characterization of the whole which is the Indian world, to an examination of its components. The Bureau of Indian Affairs is not the only federal agency involved. Others, notably the Public Health Service, increasingly play a role. But with the possible exception of the poverty program, these other departments and agencies have been absorbed into the old system without fundamentally altering it. State governments—Maine and California among them—have done no better and may have been worse in their dealings with the Indians. The following examination will focus primarily on the BIA because of its historical domination of all that is Indian: tribal government, education, job opportunities, land, economic development.

We shall look intensively at three key areas: education, health and land in which Government policies and practices have steadily eroded and disintegrated the Indian's heritage. We begin with education, that process upon which our nation's culture, political system, identity and progress ultimately rest. For the Indian, however, education is not a catalyst for self-realization and betterment, but an instrument for destruction. It is a form of war.

1

EDUCATION AS WAR

Education for the American Indian today follows a pattern of "cold war," modeled on a time-tested formula. Its components:

—Promises made and promises broken.

—The long trek from home to the white man's wasteland.

—Unremitting pressure toward total submission, leading to personal, cultural and ethnic annihilation.

Promises are cheap. A treaty signed a century ago between the United States Government and the Navajo nation included this pledge:

> "The United States agrees that for every 30 children . . . who can be induced or compelled to attend school, a house shall be provided and a teacher competent to teach the elementary branches of an English education shall be furnished. . . ."

In 1969, 40,000 Navajos—nearly a third of the entire tribe—are functional illiterates in English.

Rupert Costo, President of the American Indian Historical Society and a chairman of the Cahuilla tribe of California, says Indians have always considered education crucial to their survival. "In our contact with the whites, we have always and without fail asked for one thing. We wanted education. You can examine any treaty, any negotiations with the American whites. The first condition, specifically asked for by the Indian tribes, was education." [1]

In spite of that and in spite of periodic reassertions by the Government of its commitment to education, the product —through BIA-operated boarding schools and day schools and through contract arrangements with local public school districts—is abysmally poor.

The Bureau of Indian Affairs operates 77 boarding schools, scattered throughout the nation, and 147 day schools located on or near reservations. In recent years, the Bureau has sought to transfer much of its responsibility for educating Indian children to local school districts, entering into contracts with the states. In 1969, 57.4 per cent of all Indians attending schools were in public schools, attending classes with non-Indians. Two-thirds of the remaining youngsters, or some 35,000 children, are sent to boarding schools. BIA day schools serve only 16,000 children, or about 14 per cent of the Indians in school.

In 1966, more than 16,000 Indian children of school age were not attending any school at all.

—*The average educational level for all Indians under federal supervision is five school years.*

—*Dropout rates are twice the national average.*

—*Indian children score consistently lower than white children at every grade level, in both verbal and non-verbal skills according to national tests, administered in 1965. The longer the Indian child stays in school, the further behind he gets.*

—*More than one out of five Indian males (22.3 per cent) have less than five years of schooling.*

—*The Cherokees of Oklahoma today have reached an educational level one year behind the state's Negro population of 10 years ago and 2.2 school years behind the Negro population of present-day Oklahoma.*

It is the same bleak story, no matter whether one studies national Indian statistics, a single BIA school, or even the public schools serving Indians and receiving special federal funds. (If any distinction is to be made, the public schools receiving special BIA funds may have done even worse. The BIA has abdicated responsibility—even though its funds and its trust obligations are involved.)

The human needs of children are "swept away when [the Indian child] is put in a BIA boarding school situation, where there might be as many as 100 to 150 other children under the care of a single matron. She is supposed to provide a substitute environment to become a parent-substitute for him." [2]

"I many times stay up late at night holding a girl's head on my lap while she is crying," a boarding school staff member lamented, "but when you have 100 students in a dormitory it is impossible to comfort all those who need comforting." [3]

Senator Walter Mondale of Minnesota, a member of the Senate Indian Education Subcommittee was advised by the BIA recently that "there is one psychologist in the whole BIA [school] system and only two or three social workers." Most counselors and dormitory aides are unprepared for the difficult tasks that face them at Bureau boarding schools. They often perceive their roles as that of guards rather than substitute parents. Those few who are skilled and dedicated have little time to devote to helping the children with special

ED ECKSTEIN

problems, because of overcrowding and understaffing. One boarding school counselor said he spends most of his time retrieving AWOLs, supervising housekeeping and other "general service tasks," but spent *none* of his time counseling—even though he works a 10 to 16 hour day.

> "There is a tendency—a pronounced tendency—to 'herd' rather than guide. The boys and girls are yelled at, bossed around, chased here and there, told and untold, until it is almost impossible for them to attempt to do anything on their own initiative—except, of course, to run away." [4]

The entire BIA educational system is plagued by mediocrity: an overburdened and sometimes insensitive staff, inadequate physical facilities, out-of-date texts and supplies, little money for innovation. Teachers' salaries are not competitive with the public schools. The pay may be the same, but the BIA hires on a year-round basis requiring 12-months work while public school teachers work about 180 days a year. Educational specialists confirm the observation of a 1966 Presidential Task Force that "too many BIA employees were simply time-servers of mediocre or poor competence who remain indefinitely because they were willing to serve in unattractive posts at low rates of pay for long periods of time."

Teachers who come to the reservation day schools often know little about the children they are going to teach (only one per cent of the reservation elementary teachers are Indian). Teacher orientation and training sessions pay scant attention to Indian cultural values or to problems which the teacher may encounter with children who speak little or no English, have different values and know different experiences. Instead, orientation concentrates on housing, pay, and civil service fringe benefits.

Widely publicized innovations and crash programs have slight impact on the BIA schools. For example, an experimental program to teach English as a second language was implemented to make it easier for Indian children to learn English, but a national report has shown that the program often is ignored. One teacher left the materials untouched because she "did not believe in the new system of teaching English."

A former Assistant BIA Commissioner of Education, Dr. Carl Marburger, remarked: "The Education Division is isolated from the research, program development, evaluation and dissemination activities in education so that the educators in the Bureau are severely out of touch with the practices in the field."

> "I was in Alaska," reports Congresswoman Julia Butler Hansen of Washington, "and I saw 'John and Jane went to the store,' or 'John and Jane had a cow,' as reading examples in the textbooks. This was the Far North, just below the Arctic Circle. They had never seen a cow and they may never see a cow. . . ."

The sterility of the curriculum is typically matched by the bleakness of the facilities. Dr. Robert Bergman, a child psychiatrist with the Indian Division of the Public Health Service, noted:

> "Dormitories are usually large barrack-like structures with no provision for privacy, and usually no space that is each individual's to control as he sees fit. Only occasionally is there opportunity for the children to decide on the decoration of any of their living spaces."

At the Chilocco boarding school in Oklahoma, one dormitory room contained exposed heavy duty electrical wiring at the head of one youngster's bed. A BIA report on conditions at the school admitted, "the possibility of that girl being electrocuted in her sleep was evident." The two-room Gila River Indian Day School in Arizona is a rebuilt garage. It serves 130 children, 60 of them in a room which should hold 29.

A survey of BIA teachers in 1965 revealed that 25 per cent would rather be teaching whites than Indians. Still another survey showed that while Indian students saw jobs and college as their long-range educational priorities, their teachers believed an ability to get along and assimilation were more important traits for Indians to absorb.[5]

It was the Indian's great misfortune to be conquered by a people intolerant of cultural diversity. The Indian looked different, spoke a different language, had his own religion and customs; Americans saw him as an anathema and were chagrined when he refused to conform to "civilization." Indian education policies were formulated—in the words of a Commissioner of Indian Affairs—". . . to prepare him for the abolishment of tribal relations, to take his land in severalty and in the sweat of his brow and by the toil of his hands to carve out, as his white brother has done, a home for himself and his family." [6]

The Long Trek— from Homeland to Wasteland

The Indian child's trek to school, measured in miles, becomes a Trail of Tears, a form of compulsory and permanent expatriation, especially for the 35,309 children attending BIA boarding schools. In 1968, 9,000 of the children in Indian boarding schools were less than nine years old.

In Alaska, where 15 per cent of the national Indian population resides, there are not enough schools, nor is there room for all the Indian children in public schools. As a result, Indian children are shipped as far away as Oklahoma, 6,000 miles from their parents.

Even where the Indian children attend day schools or public schools, the journey can be a rugged one. In Utah, Indian children wake up at 4:30 a.m., walk three to four miles over rough terrain to the bus and then ride 65 miles to the public school. In New Mexico, high school students walk two miles to the bus every day, and then ride 50 miles to school.

Once in a boarding school, the children are effectively cut off from their families. Parents cannot visit often because of the great distance and because many schools are located where roads are impassable for much of the year. Boarding school officials do not offer transportation or accommodations for parents who might want to come. Even when the school is convenient to the reservations, parental visits are

discouraged because the children often become hard to man
age after parents leave and sometimes run away.

Permission to see one's own parent is not a "right." It is
often granted as a reward for good behavior—or denied as a
form of punishment. "If [the child] has been a 'problem'
(e.g. has run away) parents are often not allowed to take
him until he has 'learned his lesson.' This may take up to a
month to accomplish." [7]

Education becomes a forced journey to alien institutions: on the Navajo reservation, BIA schools are called
"Washingdoon bi oltka" which means "Washington's
schools." From the Indian's point of view, the public schools
seem the longest way from home. The Navajos refer to them
as *"Beligaana bi oltaka,"* the "little white man's schools."

The journey to school takes on many meanings. But
above all it expresses the white man's judgment of rejection
and disdain for the child's home and way of life. The message is not subtle. At one boarding school, a child was heard
to pray:

"Dear Lord, help me not to hate my mother and father."

At another, a school teacher exclaimed in a fit of anger:
"If you want to live in a hogan for the rest of your life just
don't bother to study." One student left school precisely because she did want to live in a hogan for the rest of her life.[8]

Boarding schools serve "students with marked educational retardation based on either delayed school entrance
or past social and behavioral problems, and . . . students who
have unsatisfactory home conditions or social-emotional
problems," as well as children who have no schools available
near their homes. Poverty is regarded as an unsatisfactory
home condition. Many boarding school students are welfare
referrals; the schools are used to avoid providing increased
family assistance and parents are penalized for being poor
by having their children shipped off to distant boarding institutions.

Senator Barry Goldwater showed some understanding
of the problem: "I try to picture myself as an Indian parent
and try to sense what I might feel when my child was sent

Navajo boys talking with their teacher at a school on the Reservation. PAUL CONKLIN

to school either close by or many, many miles away to a boarding school, knowing that the child would come back, yes, speaking English but also having forgotten the religion of his tribe, the ancient ways of his tribe. . . ."

The day school is just as explicit a rejection as the boarding school. Its function is to save the child from his own home and family. One school principal states bluntly:

"When the mothers ask me what they can do to help their children, I tell them: 'Don't do anything.' "

"It isn't that they should fear authority but that they should respect the authority that is doing things for their own good." 9

A Pueblo day school teacher expressly rejects the child's home by ruling it off limits professionally:

"My business and my concerns extend only as far as
this fence"—pointing to the fence around the school—
"what happens outside of these school grounds is none
of my business." [10]

*The significance, relevance, and even the existence of
the Indian world and its values is systematically denied by
school administration.* The Indian child is kept in deliberate
ignorance of his culture, history and heritage. He is taught,
simultaneously, that he should be ashamed of it.

Textbooks, in dealing with the Indian, often are appall-
ing. A history text, recently in use in California public
schools, gave this description:

"The Indians who lived in the Stanislaus area were
known as the 'Diggers,' although they were the Walla
Tribe. They were stupid and lazy and it is said they
were given their name because of their habit of dig-
ging in the earth. They dug roots for food, and they also
dug holes in the ground for shelter. The squaw was required and expected to provide all of the food for her
husband and family." [11]

The late Senator Robert F. Kennedy of New York related
this experience:

"We were in Idaho the other day and I was asking the
superintendent of schools, where they had 80 per cent
Indian children, whether they taught anything about
Indian history or Indian culture. The tribe was a very
famous tribe, the Shoshone, which had a considerable history, and he said, 'There isn't any history to
this tribe;' this has a tremendous effect on the children. So I asked him if there were any books in the library where all these children could go and read about
Indian history, and he said, 'Yes,' and we went to the library. There was only one book and the book was entitled, 'Captive of the Delawares.' It showed a white
child being scalped by an Indian."

The teachers are not trained to counteract these dis-
torted accounts of the Indian's history. In California, which
has the second largest Indian population in the country,
teacher training in the colleges devotes "something like six-
and-a-half pages of the required reading . . . to . . . Indians,

and about five-and-a-half of these six pages are very detri-
mental to the Indian child." [12]

The Lower Brule Sioux Tribe of South Dakota reports
that at their day school "students seldom hear anything
about Indian culture or history" and "pride in their heritage
is not encouraged." The Mesquakies of Iowa set up an art
class in an abandoned farmhouse when the instructors at
their day school refused to permit Indian art in the class-
rooms.

The official business of the school is teaching middle-
class values and skills to "culturally deprived children." The
BIA's *Curriculum Needs of Navajo Pupils* states that the
Navajo child:

> "Needs to begin to develop knowledge of how the dom-
> inant culture is pluralistic, and how these people worked
> to become the culture which influences the American
> mainstream of life . . ."
> "Needs to understand that every man is free to rise as
> high as he is able and willing . . ."
> "Needs assistance with accepting either the role of
> leader or follower . . ."
> "Needs to understand that work is necessary to exist
> and succeed . . ."

These "needs" are defined and centered within the
cultural universe of the non-Indian world. The possibility
that the Indian child may need an education which helps him
function as an Indian, or that Indian parents might want
such an education for their children, is not considered.

Instead of family-type cohesion based on respect, the
schools encourage market relationships to enforce rules. At
one boarding school, a program of "behavior modification"
has been instituted. A child may earn points for good behavior and use them to purchase items he may want. A can
of deodorant sells for 150 to 200 points. A frisbee, a 50-
cent toy children toss in the air, goes for 500 points. But a
child who maintains a "perfect" record can only earn 60
points in any week.

Dr. John Collier Jr., a professor of cultural anthropology at
San Francisco State College, reports of children at Chilocco,

Oklahoma Boarding School: Pervasive attacks are made against their cultural beliefs . . . teachers advocate the free labor of Navajo girls in their homes, doing laundry, scrubbing floors, etc., all done on students' after-school time, 'to teach them the American way of housekeeping.' "[13]

When an Eastern Oklahoma public school administrator was asked whether he thought English should be taught as a second language to Indian children, he blindly insisted that "only 'American' be taught in [the] schools." [14]

Struggling with English, the Indian child gradually learns how he is regarded: "dumb Indian."

> "In the public schools of today, the Cherokee student is frequently infringed against by the teacher. He is at a linguistic disadvantage in that he possibly hears and speaks only Cherokee at home. Then, when he goes to school, he has to think and talk in English. This is confusing and naturally makes his responses slower than the white student of the same mental ability. This hesitation sometimes gives rise to the oft-heard phrase 'dumb Indian,' when the Indian really is not 'dumb' at all." [15]

The main "achievement" of the schools is to provide Indian children with an educational experience designed to root out all traces of their Indian heritage. Some of the methods go back 70 years, as if time stood still for Indian education.

Dr. Bergman made these observations:

> "On the theory that 'if the children are allowed to talk Navajo, they won't bother to learn English,' native language is usually forbidden. . . .
> "In the world of the boarding school not only the Navajo language but almost all things Navajo are rated very low. The children are frequently told not to be like their parents and are often admonished against following the traditions of their people." [16]

The Indian child often encounters discrimination in the public schools. In Oklahoma, Cherokee children have been called "black rats" by the teachers.

> "A student in Ponca City asks if she has to sit by an Indian. The teacher says, 'No, I know what you mean.'

Our girls are called 'squaws.' We are greeted with, 'How.' If it rains, we are asked if we have been dancing. If we get a haircut, we are asked if they can scalp us. Everything we know and cherish is derided and made a butt of jokes." [17]

In Arizona, Indian children so poor that they come to school without breakfast have been made to work for their lunch. In Oklahoma, some children who recently graduated from high school never received their diplomas; they were ashamed to appear at the ceremony because they had no decent clothes to wear, nor could they afford to buy class rings and pictures. Isolated and separate, the Indian public school children stick to themselves, exiles in their native land.

It does not take long for the Indian child to understand the true nature of his journey. That exciting adventure of exploring a new world called "school" quickly becomes perceived as a one-way journey—to a wasteland from which there is no return.

When the Indian child enters school, he appears eager to learn.

"An observer's first impressions of the lower elementary grades (Beginners, First, Second, Third) at an Indian Day School are likely to be positive. If the teacher is fairly competent and the class small, the children appear attentive, obedient, and eager to learn." [18]

The children "jump up and answer right away" and "help out each other." They seem "enormously 'teacher oriented' " and say they "like school." Tests show that Indian children appear to achieve satisfactorily until they reach about the fourth grade level. After that, the relationship between teacher and student changes radically. Achievement scores show a steady and progressive decline. "Children of the typical rooms appear shy, withdrawn, stupid and sullen." By the seventh grade "the students have surrounded themselves with a wall of silence that is impenetrable to the outsider. . . ." [19]

Resistance begins when the Indian child is old enough to know he is Indian and conscious enough of the world around

"Eager to learn."

PAUL CONKLIN

him to understand what the school is teaching him about being Indian:

> "Indian children perceive very early what most whites think of their parents and themselves. Once past the primary grades, they approach each teacher with caution, testing her response to them; if it is negative, they quickly retreat." [20]

Passive resistance and withdrawal express the Indian's silent defiance against overwhelming odds. The Indians "tune out." Teachers rise to meet the challenge; persuasion changes to coercion. At the Lower Brule school in South Dakota, for example, "teachers persist in violating explicit Bureau rules against verbal humiliation and corporal punishment. Tongue lashings are common; order is kept in the primary grade room with the threat, often the reality, of a stick; frequently, primary grade children are forced to sit in a locked closet for punishment. School becomes a terrifying experience as well as a waste of time." [21]

The educator sees the child's behavior as changing. He even has a technical term for it: "the cross-over phenomenon." To the Indian child, it is not he who is changing—but the world into which he was welcomed, and which he entered with joy and trust.

Indian children face unremitting pressure toward submission and toward cultural annihilation. All who pass through the Indian education system become casualties— casualties of education waged as war. The casualties take many forms.

There are the dead:

Recently, two young boys froze to death while running away from a boarding school. They were trying to get to their homes—50 miles away.

Senator Mondale made this report on the Fort Hall, Idaho Reservation: "The subcommittee was told during its visit to that reservation that the suicide rate among teenagers was perhaps as high as 100 times the national average. No one really knew for certain but everyone could cite examples. We were told that suicides had occurred as early as 10 years of age."

In one school on the Northern Cheyenne Reservation, also in Montana, there were a dozen suicide attempts in 18 months, among fewer than 200 pupils.

There are the physically scarred.

At Intermountain Indian School in Utah, "unmanageable" students are regularly handcuffed and beaten. Last Fall, a student thought to be drunk and unmanageable was carted off to jail, where he committed suicide by hanging himself with his sweater. The student was actually having convulsions and needed medical attention. One school employee at Intermountain "dunks the students' head into a toilet bowl which is unfit for even a hand," whenever he suspects them of drinking.[22]

There are the psychologically scarred.

"There is not one Indian child who has not come home in shame and tears after one of those sessions in which

he is taught that his people were dirty, animal-like, something less than a human being." [23]

At a boarding school, a nervous, intense boy rose in the assembly hall and blurted out, "Let's face it, some of us are here because we haven't anywhere else to go." [24]

"A Cheyenne girl, when asked why she spent her 'hard-earned' money on liquor, replied, 'Because I am a Cheyenne, and that is the way we Cheyennes are.' " [25]

The Indian child in the 12th grade has the poorest self-concept of all minority groups tested. Dropouts among Indian children "wander around the reservation for five or six years, just doing unskilled labor, or off the reservation. I do not think anybody has any figures on this. . . ." [26]

A study: "Papago male, age 18, full Indian. Left federal boarding school 9th grade at age 17. He was in some kind of trouble at school. Later, he was sent to the federal camp in the Catalinas. After being discharged he was picked up and [sent] to a federal prison in Colorado."

"Pima boy, age 18, one-half Indian. Left public school 12th grade at age 18. Attendance and grades were poor. Now looking for work."

"Pima boy, age 16, full Indian. Left public school 9th grade at age 15. . . . He is not working. . . ."

"Papago boy, age 16, full Indian. Left public school 8th grade at age 15. Poor grades. Subsequently sent to a reform school, now released." [27]

There are the casualties which mark the slow but sure death of a culture.

Mrs. Smith was one of the first Indians on her reservation to attend public school. She dropped out before high school graduation. "I didn't like it," she remembers, "and I couldn't speak very good English." She still speaks her native language with older members of her family, but memories of her embarrassment in school made her determined never to teach her own eight children their Indian tongue.[28] An 80-year-old Shoshone Indian, Moroni Timbimboo of Weshakie, Utah, says: "Yes, we still speak in our language. But we had 20 grandchildren and seven great-grandchildren

. . . none of them speaking our language no more. They just can't understand what we are talking about."

Recently, when the Minnesota Department of Education as part of an effort to upgrade Indian education tried to find Indians willing to impart some knowledge of their history to school teachers, the Indian parents responded: "How can we? We attended the public school systems and we know nothing about our history or past. What we know we are getting on our own." [29]

Wallace L. Chafe of the Smithsonian Institution says that of about 300 recognizably separate Indian languages and dialects still extant in the United States, only roughly 40 per cent have more than 100 speakers. In the case of about 55 per cent of all these languages, the remaining speakers are of advanced age, "which implies that many of the tongues—each one an irreplaceable miracle no less than the whooping crane—are destined to disappear."

There are the educationally scarred.

If the Indian child fails, it is because he is Indian. Failure is expected, and the expectation becomes self-fulfilling. Educators hope to overcome the Indian child's cultural deprivation, but they really don't expect to succeed. Most schools are prepared to pass every Indian child, what they call "social promotions," regardless of his performance. The school insulates itself in this way from taking the blame; failure springs from cultural deprivation—not from the school. When Indian children drop out of school, stumble in learning English or withdraw into themselves, teachers call it "going back to the blanket." The phrase sums up an attitude of disdain and their definition of failure. A study at Pine Ridge Day School in South Dakota characterized the most common teacher attitude as "condescension, sometimes kindly, often well-meant, but always critical." [30] At the Chilocco, Oklahoma boarding school the staff attitude was summed up by one who said: "Well, what can you expect? These are Indian kids."

Educational failure becomes a way of life, and a method of survival.

> "Roughly half the young Sioux who leave high school very early claim they left because they were unable to conform to school regulations. What happens to the country boys who remain? Do they 'shape up' and obey the regulations? Do they, even, come to 'believe' in them? We found that most of the older and more experienced youths were, if anything, even more inclined to boast of triumphs over the rules than the younger fellows who had left. Indeed, all but one assured us that they were adept at hookey, and food and car stealing, and that they had frequent surreptitious beer parties and other outlaw enjoyments." [31]

At boarding schools, children sneak out to drink or run away. Some transfer from school to school. School records in Minnesota show that some Indian children have changed schools as many as 13 times, and up to 35 per cent will move during the school year.

The educationally scarred may be the lucky ones. They may be the least damaged. The most frightening casualties are those who have succeeded—and in doing so have lost themselves. Some achievers do make their way back. Sun Chief, a Hopi, tells his story this way:

> "As I lay on the blanket I thought about my school days and all I had learned. I could talk like a gentleman, read, write, and cipher. I could name all the states of the Union, with the capitals, repeat the names of all the books of the Bible, 100 verses of Scripture, sing more than two dozen hymns, debate, shout football yells, swing my partners, and tell dirty stories by the hour. It was important that I had learned how to get along with the white man. But my experience had taught me that I had a Hopi Spirit Guide, whom I must follow if I wish to live and I want to become a real Hopi again, to sing the old songs and to feel free to make love without the fear of sin or rawhide." [32]

Some are not so lucky. They are lost, sense it—and their words are haunting:

> "Education . . . it has separated you from your family, your heritage. . . . What more sickening life do you

want? So God help me I didn't ask for this. No, I didn't." [33]

The BIA Education System is not primarily an education system. It is best understood as a major division of the Bureau's own "military—industrial complex" which wages unrelenting war upon Indian survival.

Securing money and property becomes an end in itself; children become merely means to that end.

A study of the school system on the Pine Ridge Reservation in South Dakota concluded: "The major exhortation made by an administrator to the education committee of the Tribal Council was 'to twist the parents' arms and get them to make their children come to school.' " Administrators rewarded teachers with praise for maintaining high attendance, spoke of absent children as money out of their pockets (higher attendance means larger budget allocations and more power), felt threatened when researchers tried to check figures for attendance, and hesitated to suspend children who broke rules with impunity since it would mean fewer children on the school rosters. [34]

The education system does not exist for the sake of the children or the community; sometimes it seems to exist for its own sake, especially where acquisition of property is concerned. A piano at one boarding school is kept locked for fear the children might damage it. Bathrooms at the Pine Ridge school are locked during school hours, for, as the administrator told entering freshmen: "Once in the morning, once at noon, and after school. Only babies go more often." Day school facilities are rarely opened to the community for social affairs. A school official who did open a building one evening, to demonstrate to the community that it was "their school," felt the community showed its basic irresponsibility when minor damage was done to "his" building.

In 1953, the BIA started a crash program to provide improved educational opportunities for Navajo Indian children. Between 1953 and 1967, "supervisory positions in headquarters, area offices, and agencies increased by 112.9 per cent; supervisory positions at BIA schools increased by

144.3 per cent; general administrative and clerical positions at BIA schools increased by 93.8 per cent; while teaching positions increased by only 19.5 per cent." [35] The staff that implemented the crash program still holds office. Through the flexibility of civil service, the average age of top level (GS-14 and 15) education administrators is 58 years; the median years of BIA experience is 27 years; and of other outside experience only 4½ years.

Non-education activities which serve the bureaucracy's empire-building activities are passed off as educational expenditures. A recent study cites six administrative-type service programs which draw on education program funds. Included in the education budget were such items as maintaining order, resources management, construction of irrigation systems, and federal-aid highway road construction projects. This assessment against education funds amounted to $12,235,000 in 1967, approximately 10 per cent of the total education budget. When confronted with this, Congresswoman Hansen of Washington, chairman of a Congressional Appropriations Subcommittee, raged:

> "For the people wanting to economize, they will look at the cost of educating an Indian child as against the cost of educating somebody in the public schools. We are not writing off against the public school budget the administration of the town hall. . . . You see the difficulties you get into. It is going to hurt your education program eventually, because as these increase, this 10 per cent looks very high. . . . The soul of an accountant shouldn't run education. I am going to be very blunt on that."

Recently, the Government Accounting Office reviewed BIA housing construction for school employees undertaken over a seven-year period. [36] In Arizona and New Mexico, the GAO reviewed 752 out of 1,322 units, and concluded that about 350 units costing $5 million were not justified or needed to meet the Bureau's housing requirements. GAO said another 220 units out of 274 constructed at seven school facilities located near communities and costing about $3.2 million also were not justified or needed. Another 130 of 478 units constructed in isolated areas, built at a cost of $1.8 million, also were criticized. GAO concluded, "This [construction] resulted primarily because the Bureau had not administered its employee housing construction program in accordance with the policies and standards established by the [Bureau of the Budget]." As part of its review, GAO discovered that a considerable number of housing units in different school areas were occupied by BIA employees not connected with the operation of the school and by individuals not employed by the BIA.

Education funds also are spent on supplies which are not needed, wanted or used, which results in the accumulation of inventory as an end in itself.[37] GAO found that Navajo area schools in the Southwest were ordering supplies without reference to stocks on hand. Nine schools had purchased supplies valued at $124,650 in excess of need, enough to last up to 38 years. At six of the schools, 20,883 unused books were in storage, and the purchase of an additional 1,390 books had been approved. GAO found that 3,073 books on hand were not being used because there was no program at the schools requiring them.

The GAO found instances where equipment had been purchased for a school even though serviceable items could have been obtained from other schools.[38] For example, at the Fort Wingate, New Mexico elementary school, 18 sewing machines were stored in a basement, five of them still packed in the manufacturer's shipping cartons. At the Thoreau School in New Mexico, GAO found an overhead projector and a duplicating machine packed in cartons and an order showing that the equipment was purchased two years earlier.

Much equipment on hand was allowed to remain in an unserviceable condition. GAO found that at two schools, "73 equipment items, with recorded values totalling about $11,200 . . . had remained unserviceable for extended periods . . ." up to two years.

The Government Accounting Office's review of BIA school construction showed that large sums had been programmed and expended to repair, improve, and rehabilitate old buildings. [39] Some of these old buildings were demolished a short time later and others are scheduled for demolition in the near future. For example, the BIA spent over $80,000 to repair a boys' dormitory from 1960 through 1964, only to raze the building in 1965. The kitchen-dining hall at Fort Wingate School in New Mexico was repaired for $70,000 during 1960 through 1962. In 1963, the building was abandoned.

Education funds also are siphoned off for capital investment in obsolete plants and obsolete approaches. Despite official policy decisions dating back 40 years to move away from the boarding school concept and toward day schools, the Bureau continues to make large investments in building new boarding schools and rehabilitating old ones, deepening its financial commitment to the boarding school approach. The boarding school program has been under attack since 1928. Yet in 1967 and 1968, half the construction budget went into building new and fixing old boarding school facilities.

The BIA justifies building boarding schools by citing a shortage of access roads in rural areas on the reservations. A separate division of the BIA builds roads, but no effort has been made to coordinate road construction with school location.

Plans are underway to refurbish the dilapidated school of Chemawa, Oregon. The children at Chemawa are shipped there from Alaska because there is no room for them in schools at home. Instead of building more schools in Alaska, the BIA is repairing Chemawa and perpetuating the practice of shipping children 6,000 miles to school.

Recently, the Navajo Tribal Council passed a resolution asking the BIA to build boarding schools nearer to the reservation so that children could be educated closer to home. Two new facilities are now under construction on the reservation. At the same time, the BIA is constructing a new facility at Riverside, California for boarding students, 70 percent of whom are Navajo children from the Southwest.

"As far as construction of schools are [concerned]," a representative of the Navajo tribe reports, ". . . they just build them anywhere they wish. . . . They build these big institutions. . . . There is lots of empty space, so they round up these kids and fill them up. The demand is there, they think that Congress is going to get after them because they don't fill those spaces. And so, Toyei School (Arizona) isn't filled yet, so they are going to come around and take some more of these little bitty ones to fill that school so they can keep the Congress happy."

At the Budget Bureau, former Assistant Commissioner Marburger recalled, "They continually make odious comparisons with local school districts where Indian children are also often receiving an inadequate education without recognizing the formidable additional handicap of isolation, language and family problems of the children in boarding schools."

The BIA per-pupil cost is much higher than the nation-wide average of $536 per-pupil. As a result, Bureau officials have been forced to argue that this is not a fair comparison. They have blamed the Indian child, classifying him as "culturally deprived" and therefore in need of special expenditures, like the handicapped and retarded. That rationale shifts the blame for failure to the child. And it avoids any honest examination in terms of expenditures and results.

The Bureau of Indian Affairs continues waging educational war against the Indian children. Its methods haven't changed.

Educational goals are subordinated to the accumulation of power as an end in itself.

Substantive educational policy is consistently subordinated and professional decisions are thwarted and subverted by the overriding concern of the larger bureaucratic establishment. Those who control Indian education policy are neither Indians nor educators. It is the responsibility of non-educators—mostly land administrators—to whom the educators are subject in the BIA line of command. The Assistant Commissioner for Education, second-ranking official within the BIA, does not even control his own line staff. Dr. Marburger, a respected educator, took office in April 1966 and remained only 15 months. He left in frustration after realizing that his policies were not followed down the line, and that he could not even obtain information from the field.

"There was not a flagrant disobedience of orders or anything of the sort," Dr. Marburger said, "but just a failure for things to happen." Personnel decisions, construction and rehabilitation projects and data processing fell under other assistant commissioners or directors, and attempts to bring in new blood or innovate were thwarted by a lack of access and lack of control over personnel. "I would find out that so-and-so had been promoted and I was not aware of it. The channels were there, but it just didn't happen quite that way."

In December 1968, Leon Osview, an educational consultant from Temple University, pointed out that the Assistant Commissioner of Education in the BIA was doomed to failure because at the Washington level he could be overpowered by other assistant commissioners in charge of budget, administration and long range program planning. In the field, he exercises no vertical control over his own education staff. Osview commented, "Under present circumstances I, for example, wouldn't take his job for either love or money. . . . My impression is that the Bureau is spongy enough to absorb almost any amount of criticism."

Osview notes that educational decisions are, in fact, made by non-educators, by administrative officers, and that the decentralized structure of the BIA renders headquarters officials powerless to effect change: "[N]o one is in much doubt that it is the Area Directors who make or break the Bureau."

Purposeful insulation from professional criticism or external review is built in the BIA makeup. The Bureau has built up a series of offensive and defensive weapons to attack or discredit those who are critical of educational performance—and to suppress or render ineffectual both criticism and constructive efforts to improve the educational system—and finally to eliminate clear lines of responsibility and accountability so that it is never possible to affix blame or hold any single official accountable for its failures.

Nowhere has this been better illustrated than in Chilocco, Oklahoma. For years there were rumors of BIA staff members abusing students at the Chilocco boarding school. In late 1968 the BIA sent investigators to the school. They found evidence of criminal malpractice among the teachers and school officials, and reported it to the Interior Department's top official for Indian matters, Theodore Taylor. Taylor asked for a full report.

The report was written, but no action was taken until early April 1969, when the report was leaked to Senator Lee Metcalf of Montana. Metcalf exposed the Chilocco conditions in a Senate floor speech and, at a hearing on April 23, he chided BIA education commissioner Charles Zellers: "It seems you would have done something."

Only after Metcalf's outcry was anything done to alleviate conditions. The school's superintendent was suspended. From the time the investigation was ordered, however, retaliatory measures had begun against officials working to change Chilocco. Once out of office, BIA education commissioners have admitted that their proposals for change, their demands for information, and their policy mandates often went nowhere. (A summer 1969 FBI report denied physical abuse at Chilocco.)

Criticism and change is thwarted at the bottom, as well as at the top. A plaintive expression of this frustration came from a teacher in a letter to the late Senator Kennedy:

> "Finally, please don't bother to send this letter on to the BIA, as I wrote you last year and the letter came back 'down the line' to the local level, and the very people involved in some of the situations described here evaluated themselves and their programs. The only thing that came out of that were some dark days for me, and a label as a troublemaker.
>
> "I'd like to, someday, be able to work my way up to a position where I could change things—that would be hard to do if I'm on my superiors' [black] list. . . ." [40]

Staff members of the Carnegie Cross Cultural Project, examining Indian education in Oklahoma, found themselves subjected to ostracism and professional defamation.

Staff members of Congressmen who are suspected of being critical of the Bureau meet similar obstacles—though they are treated more deferentially. Overt attacks are channeled by the Bureau through tribal spokesmen. In anticipation of a forthcoming congressional field staff trip, officials at the Albuquerque Boarding School hastily purchased and distributed teddy bears and drapes for the children's dormitories.

Today the Bureau seeks to absolve itself from responsibility for failure by contracting out its responsibility to public schools. Under the 1934 Johnson-O'Malley Act the BIA receives funds for the purpose of contracting with the states to provide education for Indian children. The BIA exacts no special commitments in exchange for these funds. The states simply ignore the special needs of Indians while using Indian funds to subsidize the total state school system. In 1968, 57.4 per cent of all school-age Indians attended public schools.

The record of state public schools in educating Indians with special BIA funds is sometimes worse than the BIA's. The BIA points to their failure to show that BIA schools are superior—and indirectly to imply that its failures are the fault of the Indian and not of the Bureau. In this manner, the Bureau buys political support from state education agencies permitting its money to be used to subsidize the normal operating costs of the public schools, to increase the state education budget—but not to provide specialized quality education for Indians.

"In New Mexico, neither the Bureau nor the State Board of Education make suggestions as to how the Johnson-O'Malley funds should be used. The local boards . . . spend the money as they wish. The annual reports about Johnson-O'Malley money from the states do not explain how the money is used." [41]

Osview, in examining public school education of Indian children, commented:

"I was shocked to find that BIA does not, apparently as a matter of policy, engage in any *programmatic* co-operation with public school people, of whose desire and willingness to do justice to their Indian students there can be no doubt. BIA knows about Indian children, or if they don't, they should. Public schools don't and can't really be expected to, on their own."

In the BIA's educational operations there is no accountability to the Indian. The Bureau resists at every point any steps which would make Bureau employees and Bureau-paid educators directly accountable to the Indians. In 1968 President Johnson issued a message of Indian Affairs: "I am directing the Secretary of the Interior to establish Indian school boards for Federal Indian schools."

The BIA's response has been to establish education advisory boards. The advisory boards are not elected and they are just that—advisory. They have no power over funding, hiring, or over the general direction of Indian educational policy. Former Assistant Commissioner Marburger called the advisory boards "a phony . . . like a student council."

Even where there is an Indian school board, it is kept powerless, manipulated by the Bureau school superintendent. Where Indians make up a majority of a school board, as has happened on rare occasions on the Navajo reservation, "the superintendent plays the dominant role and meetings are characterized principally by Navajo acquiescense and very little participation." They are "not aware of their potential responsibilities and areas of influence." [42] This is no accident. Attempts to secure some degree of control and accountability are ignored or are met with swift retaliation.

"Over at Steamboat," relates Annie Wauneka, a Navajo representative, ". . . they had a problem with the Bureau school, and there was certain personnel, the top official, the top echelon which means the superintendent, the principal, and so forth—the community didn't like these individuals. They were unfair to the employees, they were unfair to the community. . . . We have a chapter meeting, and we call this grassroot organization. . . . So, they voted there at the chapter meeting, 171 to 0, none opposed, asking that the responsible people . . . at the area office . . . to transfer these individuals out and replace them with somebody else who they can work with. We were unsuccessful. They said civil service regulations say we can't move these people unless you have facts to show us what is wrong with these people. Well, we are beaten just like on the television, the Indians are always beaten."

Similarly, where Indians are enrolled in state public schools no attempt has been made to give Indians a meaningful voice in the way in which their children are being treated in the public schools. The Bureau takes a hands-off policy.

Robert A. Roessel, Jr., former director of the Rough Rock Demonstration School in Arizona, noted that "on the Navajo reservation . . . public schools which reservationwide enroll over 80 per cent Navajo students are in every instance controlled by school boards whose membership is over 50 per cent non-Indian."

In Oklahoma, one school has a 100 per cent Indian enrollment and a three-man, non-Indian school board. In California, where 80,000 Indians reside and the children attend public schools, there is no Indian representation on the State Advisory Commission on Education.

Such figures indicate the promise of Indian education has not been met after three centuries.

It was in 1792 that Cornplanter, negotiating for the Senecas, asked President George Washington to make education a provision of the peace treaty:

> "Father, you give us leave to speak our minds concerning the tilling of the ground. We ask you to teach us to plough and to grind corn; that you will send smiths among us, and above all, that you will teach our children to read and to write, and our women to spin and to weave."

That was the first of many requests and many promises. They were not honored then. They are not honored now. The Indians are still waiting.

II

WHITE MAN'S MEDICINE: THE INDIAN AND THE PUBLIC HEALTH SERVICE

Preserving the health of the American Indian is not a duty of the BIA. That responsibility was taken from the Bureau in 1955 in an effort to increase the resources and upgrade the prestige, efficiency and calibre of medical care for Indians. The Division of Indian Health of the U.S. Public Health Service (PHS) was created to fill the need, and PHS today appears to stand outside and above the all encompassing relationship between the BIA and the Indian.

Within the context of the Indian world, the health services which are provided appear satisfactory. Not because the Indian is healthy; on the contrary, his health status is as bad, comparatively as his educational and economic situation. But because PHS appears so alert and businesslike, it appears an exception to the low standards usually reserved for Indians.

The exception, however, is no exception. Despite its seeming autonomy, its greater professionalism, its specific achievements here and there, PHS is an integral part of the system which tends to destroy Indians and the Indian world. As the education system has failed to educate, so the Public Health Service has failed to bring health, in any meaningful sense, to the Indian. "The health level of the American Indian," President Johnson observed recently, "is the lowest of any major population group in the United States."

PHS seeks to deal in concrete terms: broken arms mended, tuberculosis diagnosed and treated, diseases cured or pain eased. It tends to stay aloof from matters of policy, from questions of culture, from the intimacies of Indian life.

Its worries center around money, supplies and staff.

Yet the fundamental health indices among the Indians do not depend solely on more doctors, more treatments, more pills and serums. So long as PHS preoccupies itself with crisis-oriented, individual medical treatment, it will be unable to significantly alter the overall low health conditions of the Indian people. At present the Public Health Service offers inadequate preventive care, shows little interest in the underlying causes of Indian ill-health, and is making no notable progress in delivering health services to the remote rural areas where Indians reside. Present priorities and policies put temporary relief for the few at the expense of life and health for the many. Basic Indian health levels remain incredibly low.

Like the educational system, Indian health care has the effect of a form of cultural war. Indians often must reject their traditions to secure the white man's medicine—a more-than-metaphoric choice between life and death. The Indian submits, but submission is not surrender. As the Indian child thwarts his BIA teachers with failure and by dropping out, so the Indian resists white man's medicine with alcoholism, with suicide and with accidents that are thinly disguised efforts at self-destruction. In this many-faceted war between cultures, the PHS—like the BIA educators—pursues a policy of health care in which the Indian is an object, not a participant.

Indians have the highest infant mortality rate in the nation: 32.2 of every 1,000 Indian babies born on the reservations die during their first year, compared to 23.7 per 1,000 nationally. On some reservations the rate ranges to 100 deaths per 1,000 births—roughly twice as many as in the worst Negro ghettoes in the nation, and four times the death rate among white babies.

The life expectancy of Indians on the reservation is nearly one-third shorter than the national average: 44 years compared to 64 years. Alaskan natives die, on the average, by the age of 35 years. Indians are afflicted with all major diseases to a much greater degree than other Americans. The

An Arizona White River Apache child with then untreated Impetigo.
BOB ADELMAN

Indian mortality rate from influenza and pneumonia is double the national average. It is the leading cause of death for Indian infants. Tuberculosis finds seven times as many victims among Indians than nationally; among Alaska Indians it is 24 times as high. The tuberculosis death rate among Indians exceeds the national rate by 500 per cent.[1]

Rare diseases are not rare among Indians. Neither is hunger, malnutrition nor mental illness.

Otitis media and other forms of ear infection, which often bring a loss of hearing, are the leading illnesses among

Indians; some 80 per cent of all Alaskan native children suffer from these diseases, and as many as one-fourth of the Eskimos in some areas of the state suffer hearing impediments. Trachoma and eye illnesses which can bring blindness, in one recent year alone, infected over 3,600 Indians on the reservations. More than half of these were under 14 years of age.

Indians suffer more pervasively from hunger and malnutrition than any group in the United States. Kwashiorkor, an extreme protein deficiency, marasmus, a wasting away of body tissues caused by calorie and protein deprivation, and other acute and fatal nutritional diseases are frequently diagnosed on reservations. Mental illness thrives at an alarming rate. Suicide, alcoholism, glue, paint and gasoline sniffing, delinquency and broken homes all are considerably more common among Indians than among the general population. Accidents, cirrhosis of the liver (attributable to excessive drinking), homicide and suicide accounted for 222 deaths per 100,000 population among Indians in 1964, nearly triple the national rate. In a 10-year-period this death rate rose 22.5 per cent among Indians. Suicide is the second leading cause of death, at a rate three times as great as among all Americans, for Indian youngsters in the 15 to 19-year-old age group.[2]

In spite of these consistently high statistics, there has been a marked decline in the morbidity and mortality rates of certain diseases. Improved hospital facilities, the greater availability of services, introduction of new drugs all have benefitted the Indian somewhat, as they have helped all Americans. Health conditions once were even worse.

The most dramatic improvement has been made in fighting tuberculosis. It now is far less frequent and also less frequently fatal than 15 years ago, largely because of new drugs. Death from intestinal diseases also has declined sharply. Mortality rates for influenza and pneumonia have dropped slightly. Infant mortality rates have dropped sharply because an increased number of Indian babies are born in hospitals. There has been no equivalent decline in infant deaths once the infant leaves the hospital and returns home.

Much of the improvement is a credit to the PHS. Since it assumed responsibility, federal spending for Indian health care has more than quadrupled, to $94 million in 1969, plus another $18 million for construction of facilities. The number of physicians has increased from 125 in 1955 to 449 in 1969. The total staff has increased from 3,574 to 6,273. The rate of growth is considerably higher than the rate of increase for BIA services largely because the Public Health Service enjoys wide support in Congress and can present expert and forceful cases for its budgets each year. A former Bureau of the Budget official commented, "The difference between the aggressive presentation of the PHS and the defensive supplications of the BIA is really something to see."

Compared to the BIA, the Public Health Service has superior professional prestige and ability to secure highly competent doctors and medical personnel. The personnel of the PHS by and large hold independent, professional status of some kind—physicians, dentists, public health nurses, nutritionists, medical social workers. Turnover is high but because of the military draft there is a steady influx of recent graduates of medical schools, trained in the most advanced and recent medical techniques.

The shortage of resources remains a major problem in the provision of quality health services to the Indians. Medical personnel is in short supply: one doctor to every 900 Indians; one dentist to every 2,900 Indians. Public Health doctors now may see 50 to 100 patients each day and thus can spend no more than five or six minutes with each examination, while an adequate examination—particularly when one must speak through an interpreter—would require at least 30 minutes.

The shortage of hospital facilities also is critical. At the Anchorage, Alaska, Native Health Service Hospital alone, there is a waiting list of 5,000 patients for major reconstructive ear surgery.[3] Many Indians travel 90 miles to a hospital clinic, only to find 200 to 300 people in line ahead of them, and leave at the end of the day without seeing a doctor. The

PHS estimates that in 1966 only one third of the total beneficiary population received dental examinations and that less than a fourth of those who needed treatment received it.

To make matters worse, the Public Health Service's resources—nurses and other supportive staff—were cut back one-sixth by Congress in 1968. Still, PHS operates as if all the health problems of the Indian are attributable solely to lack of time, money and manpower. In a review before the House Interior Committee in 1967, PHS officials said "a 40 per cent increase in personnel is required to raise the quality of the current program to the standard available to the general public."

The Indian is not "the general public." He is a special case. It is the Public Health Service tendency to operate in isolation from the environmental, cultural and personal differences of the Indians that dooms their efforts and brings about a reversal of effect. In its seemingly neutral, scientific approach to Indian culture, the Public Health Service becomes an unwitting partner in a total assault on a people and a way of life.

> "The fate of the population's health is closely intertwined with issues that have not been identified primarily as health issues. Realistically, health cannot be considered apart from environmental, social and economic influences. Personal and environmental health services are inextricably intertwined." [4]

A purely medical-clinical approach to combating disease can be futile: the incidence of such environment-related diseases among Indians actually has risen during the past decade, although medical services and resources were being sharply increased. For example, between 1962 and 1965, the incidence of otitis media increased 68 per cent, gastroenteritis 20 per cent, pneumonia 29 per cent, and streptococcal sore throat 85 per cent. [5]

Crisis-oriented medical treatment for extreme cases will never alter fundamental health levels. It can at best only postpone death and retard the rate of physical degeneration— until the patient returns home. Yet, as a matter of priority,

Sioux Indian woman in her house at Ft. Thompson Reservation in South Dakota. With no electricity or running water, the house is typical of many others on the reservation.   ED ECKSTEIN

professional preference and administrative convenience, the Public Health Service has opted to concentrate its resources on temporary cures rather than attacking underlying, environmental and nutritional causes. Its "jurisdiction" thus excludes housing, food, and transportation, and only in a limited manner has it become concerned with polluted water and waste disposal facilities.

A former head of the PHS Division of Indian Health,

Dr. C. J. Wagner, told a House Subcommittee in 1963 that more than 80 per cent of all reservation Indians had to haul drinking water a mile or more and that 78 per cent of all Indian homes obtained their water from contaminated or potentially contaminated sources, "frequently an irrigation ditch or a pond that is used with equal frequency by both the animals that he serves or takes care of and himself." Waste disposal facilities frequently consist of a primitive privy, shared among neighbors. In most areas, sanitary facilities built by PHS have not significantly altered these conditions, which are casually related to the high rates of disease and death.

PHS has no outreach system or delivery system, no systematic preventive care program, no early detection system. Thus, the Public Health Service is not structured to cope at the right point and on the proper scale with the underlying causes of poor health.

This is not unique to Indian health, but its absence is acutely noticeable on the reservations. Our health system too often does not incorporate the necessary measures to prevent disease and eliminate its underlying causes: poor housing, inadequate sanitation, malnutrition. The situation is worse on the reservations. One agency, PHS, provides the doctors, nurses and hospitals, while another agency, the BIA, builds the roads and the housing, provides the transportation and distributes the food—but the two agencies rarely coordinate efforts.

The Public Health Service serves only those who somehow make it to the hospital alive. It only pays for ambulance service if the Indian arrives alive. The weak, the lame, and the poor often do not make it that far. Sporadically, the PHS tells the BIA that Indians have a transportation problem. The BIA responds: There is no transportation problem —only a lack of roads. The problem is defined out of existence. Yet, the average cost to a Navajo to get from his reservation in central New Mexico to the Tuba City Indian hospital is $5, paid to those on the reservation who have cars.

On the Pine Ridge Reservation in South Dakota, the cost to get to a hospital runs as high as $20.

Some families on the Navajo reservation live 50 miles from the nearest improved road. PHS hospital service radii extend 70 to 90 miles. Emergency ambulance service is virtually non-existent, and anyway, the Indians lack telephones to call for help.

The *New York Times* of February 19, 1969, reported on a Navajo woman who walked 30 miles from her hogan to the nearest traveled road, carrying her sick baby. The article noted that last year 20 infants were dead on arrival at medical stations on the western half of the Navajo reservation. Eighteen of those 20 died en route, their deaths attributed to delay in reaching medical aid.

It took 36 hours last year for a Navajo mother to reach a hospital from her home, where her baby had swallowed a whole bottle of aspirin. One hour more would have been too late, the doctor said.

PHS itinerant services and field health offices are woefully inadequate. The Wanblee, South Dakota community, 90 miles from the PHS hospital at Pine Ridge, is visited once each Thursday by one doctor and two nurses. They are greeted, usually, by no fewer than 50 waiting patients. "Obviously the people do not get sick only on Thursday," one Indian complained, but even at that Wanblee fares better than most Indian communities. The Havasupai Tribe of northern Arizona said in a 1966 report that it was visited by a doctor only once every three weeks, and had no service from PHS nurses. The Confederated Tribes of the Goshute Reservation in Utah reported visits by a doctor and a nurse just once each month, from a PHS hospital 275 miles away.

The PHS contracts with 300 state and private hospitals and 400 private physicians to provide emergency and specialty services to Indians where PHS facilities are unavailable. But here, too, there are problems. Indians often are treated with contempt and rudeness. Indians fear that the Public Health Service will not pay for care at the non-PHS facility. There is a reluctance among the Indians to go to distant private hospitals, where families often cannot visit and interpreters are not available to those who do manage to make the trip. A PHS staff report notes, "Many local communities and some states seem unwilling to recognize the Indian as a citizen of a community or state entitled to the same rights and privileges as any other citizen. . . ." [6] Indians know to expect discrimination, exclusion and inferior service.

The fragmentation of authority and rivalry between the PHS Department of Indian Health and the BIA is one more aspect of the Indian's lack of power. He is unable to compel responsiveness from those ostensibly paid to serve him. The staff of the House Appropriations Committee in 1968 revealed the seriousness of this lack of coordination and communication:

> "The staff found several instances in which communications between DIH and BIA [were] practically nil. At one large boarding school, there was a mild strep throat epidemic among BIA students, being treated by DIH in the health center next to the BIA school office, but BIA officials had not been notified. A DIH official at this facility advised there was virtually no communications with BIA." [7]

Overseas, the Public Health Service units provide medical services, disseminate scientific knowledge and distribute medicine, taking the greatest care to respect local traditions and health-care functions performed by traditional leaders. On the Indian reservation this is not always the case. It often proceeds as if the medicineman, the midwife, and other tribal arrangements for caring for the sick did not exist. The effect is to communicate disdain for the accumulated skills, wisdom and sensitivity of a tradition, undermining a tribal leadership role and destroying part of a people's sense of identity and pride.

Such intolerance is self-defeating. It eliminates a potential source of medical manpower when the need is acute and when traditional health roles could clearly encompass such functions as early detection, referral, diagnostic screening, follow-up treatment and home care.

Where such PHS treatment gaps occur they attack the Indian's conception of health as bound up with his relation to his family, his community and to the moral order of the universe. A scientific, drug oriented, biochemical approach to health constitutes an assault upon a culture where people define themselves in terms of their relationship to others, where they view illness as a sign of being out of harmony with the universe.

Mrs. Annie Wauneka, a member of the Navajo Tribal Council, explains:

"Today, when a Navajo becomes ill, he must choose between the white man's doctor and his own medicine man. He has to decide which one will cure him. In the past, the Navajo people did not believe in the spread of disease, and this is still true today with a majority of them.

"There is no word for 'germ' in our language. This makes it hard for the Navajo people to understand sickness. . . ."[8]

VISTA doctor on one year's assignment to isolated Apache village in Arizona. 20 miles away on the other side of a mountain is the nearest hospital.   BOB ADELMAN

By neglecting the Indian's conception of heatlh, the PHS in effect makes scientific knowledge and medicine available only if the Indian will choose impersonal isolated treatment.

"It is very hard for the Navajo, especially the older ones who have tuberculosis, to go far from home, because they have never been off the reservation or far from their loved ones.

"A hospital is totally strange to them—strange people, strange food, strange ways of treating the sick. Bathing facilities, running water, electric lights, and thermometers are all strange. . . .

"All this must be explained. Such foods as vegetables, fish, chicken, or pork are not part of the regular Navajo diet; so this is something else they must learn. The value of these foods must be explained, as well as the value of the drugs and treatment the doctor recommends." [9]

There is no need to exact the price of alienation in exchange for the most advanced scientific treatments. The medicineman has skills and sensitivities which the Public Health Service acknowledges, particularly his diagnostic acumen. The BIA and PHS also have failed to train Indians as doctors. They have managed to train a number of female nurses, but they are non-leadership figures, unable to function within the sphere of tribal acceptance which the medicineman has known.

The Public Health Service denies any role—or voice— to Indians in the setting of health priorities, or the design and implementation of health programs.

Verbally, the Public Health Service acknowledges the necessity of planning the health program in close consultation with the Indian:

". . . I think we can state without equivocation the fact that every significant health advancement the Indian has achieved has been where the Indian himself is taking the primary responsibility for planning and assuming a job in that health endeavor. The sanitation and water supply construction program, everywhere the Indian has taken a very active role in planning these, it has been successful; where the Indian didn't take it and where we went into the reservation and put it on there without any consultation with the Indian, it has been completely valueless." [10]

Policy and practice vary widely in the Public Health Service. One PHS psychiatrist, Carl E. Mindell, has admitted:

"We really don't believe it is important to involve the people we are serving in the provision of the service. We fail to talk with them enough as equals which, of course, means our seeing that they have something to contribute to the relationship, and allowing them to make mistakes." [11]

III

INDIAN LAND—
A DWINDLING ASSET

Indian land belongs to the Indians. It is private, not public property. It is land to be used or exploited by the Indian, not the white man. It is the Indian's principal, though dwindling asset.

Land is the basis of all things Indian. It is also the basis of nearly all the BIA's activities, since the Bureau's authority as trustee of Indian land is the source of its pervasive control over all that stems from territorial dominion.

Land, moreover, has many meanings for the Indian. The relationship of a tribe to its land defines that tribe: its identity, its culture, its way of life, its fundamental rights, its methods of adaptation, its pattern of survival. Land also defines the Indian's enemies—those who covet the land and desire to expropriate it for their own use. Because Indian land is, or may be, of value, it has been, and remains, the source of almost every major conflict and every ongoing controversy between the Indian and the white man. Indian land is synonomous with Indian existence. A tribe's title to land often proves to be its death warrant.

We deal here with five definitions of land.

I. The Surveyor's Definition—The land base in terms of acres, meters, milestones and boundaries.

II. The Economist's Definition—Land as a present source of subsistence, food, shelter and income for survival.

III. The Economic Developer's Definition—Land as the basis for future economic and social self-sufficiency, as the legacy which the present bequeaths to the future, the birthright of one's children and the economic surety of future survival.

IV. The Conservationist's Definition—Land as a resource to be protected for its beauty and utility and to be prudently used and developed.

V. The Holy Man's Definition—The land embodied in a sacred relationship between man and his universe; land not to be defiled, desecrated or cheapened.

With respect to each of these dimensions, there has been systematic deprivation and expropriation. The land has been eroded, plundered, misused and spoiled. It is the Indian's only real possession. Its destruction assures the destruction of the Indian.

The Surveyor's Definition— The Land as Acreage

Between the years 1887 and 1966 the Indian land base has decreased from 138 million acres to 55 million acres. Indian land remains the subject of continual and unrelenting expropriation—most frequently in the name of progress.

Indian land is cheaper, easier and less dangerous, politically to take. So it is taken. Construction engineers, road builders and dam erectors have an uncanny knack for discovering that the only feasible and economical way to do what must be done will, unfortunately, necessitate taking the Indian's land. These principles always apply:

1) that private property interests must give way to larger considerations of public policy and social needs, and

2) that such a yielding should be structured to minimize the harm to private interests in general and to protect the interests of the majority. "The Greater Good" always hobbles the Indian. When a choice must be made as to whose private property will be taken for public purposes—an Indian's land or a non-Indian's—the Indian is invariably the loser.

Such was the case with the Indians of Fort Berthold, North Dakota in their fight to keep the United States Army Corps of Engineers from flooding their land. The opening of Garrison Dam in the spring of 1953 was a final, bitter de-

George Gillette, Chairman of Ft. Berthold Indian Tribal Business Council, weeps over 1948 sale of 155,000 acres of reservation land for Garrison Lake and Reservoir Project. Gillette said, "The Members . . . sign this contract with heavy hearts. . . ."

DEL ANKERS PHOTOGRAPHERS

feat over the Three Affiliated Tribes which for six years fought its construction. The dam flooded one-fourth of their reservation, 154,000 acres.

Although wary when reclamation officials at the Interior Department first told them what the Army had in mind, the Indians decided to settle the problem reasonably and within the purview of the law. Experts in the Bureau of Reclamation had drawn up an alternative to Garrison Dam which achieved the same purposes, inundated less valuable land, was equally feasible, and which required no intrusion on Indian treaty rights. After a series of consultations, the Army and the Interior Department led the Indians to believe the alternative would be accepted. It wasn't.

In response the Indians scraped together money and hired their own experts to devise a third plan. The tribes even offered to donate the lands they would lose to this dam—saving the government time and money—but the BIA would not endorse the plan. The Bureau of Indian Affairs received orders from the Secretary of Interior to refrain from involving the Department in further controversies with the Corps. The Army refused to consider the Indian offer.

When it became apparent that the Indians would resist the dam-building, the Government promised to provide 150,000 substitute acres of land downstream—land of equal value. The Indians were unenthusiastic. Fort Berthold was their ancestral home; further, the site for Garrison Dam had been declared unsafe by a Corps of Engineers study. Once the Indian lands had been taken and the reservation flooded, the Government "forgot" its offer. The Indians were left with no substitute land whatsoever.

The Army flooded the tribes' most fertile bottom lands, which were the basis of the entire reservation's economy. Left untouched were the harsh upland plains, barren for lack of water and with temperatures that reach 40° below zero. Beyond this, the site for the dam and the reservoir was so chosen that the waters partitioned a unified, compact territory (inhabited by a relatively prosperous cattle-raising people) into five divided and unlinkable sectors.

As at many other reservations, land at Fort Berthold had, years before the Garrison Dam crisis, been divided and parceled out in fractions among the Indians, and some had been acquired by non-Indians. Although a survey showed that 80 per cent of the Indians wished to remain on their reservation, the flooding forced many to move and the checkerboarding of the land severely limited the Indians' farming and cattle-raising. The Government promised a consolidation program, but never delivered.

So the Indians went to Washington seeking justice, with the BIA opting for a quick and minimal settlement. In the original negotiations, they were promised access to the Court of Claims should the ultimate award prove inadequate. After much negotiating, they received only $12,605,625, no mineral or other use rights were retained, and future access to the Court of Claims was denied. Five years after the Indians gave up the lands, a rich oil deposit was discovered. They received no royalties.

Relocation of the Indians was carried out by the Army

without regard for community or family, in alphabetical order. Kinship groups and native villages were dispersed. An early promise that the construction of the dam would assure lower electricity rates was never fulfilled. Wells which the Army drilled for the Indians turned black and brackish; the water was unusable. Indians were forced to buy water at 25 cents a barrel and haul it for miles.

After relocation was complete, the Bureau of Indian Affairs decided unilaterally to donate sections of Indian lands to churches and private schools. Without appraisal, the Bureau announced it would pay the tribe only $2.50 per acre for the land it seized and gave away. In 1968, a federal court found that this action violated the Indians' rights under the first and fifth amendments of the Constitution.

Today, 16 years after the opening of Garrison Dam, Fort Berthold is still in emotional and economic shock. In an effort to reestablish the old communities, tribal members travel up to 120 miles each weekend to attend reservation pow-wows, where tents are clustered along the lines of the old settlements. Unemployment stands at 60 per cent. As of 1968, welfare payments have jumped to $573,022. Prior to Garrison, however, welfare costs were never over $5,000 for any year. Life styles have been destroyed. An older member of the tribe lamented, "We seem to need to be told what to do, like children. We have been made dependent. As Bureau of Indian Affairs personnel change, we get changes in policies. . . . We sort of wait to see how the new policy will go and we go with it. A generation seems caught. The old way is gone, but there is no adequate employment for a new way."

What happened in North Dakota is not unique. The catalogue of instances in which Indian land has been taken for the public good extends to California, Arizona, Idaho, Montana, New York, South Dakota, Pennsylvania and elsewhere. Indian communities have been sacrificed to flood, irrigation and hydroelectric projects. But public works is not the only device used for seizing the Indian's land.

It has been taken to create national monuments and

parks, despite the fact that the land often is the tribe's most valuable recreational asset. A contemporary example: even now the National Park Service, which is part of the Department of the Interior, is seeking to obtain the spectacular Badlands of the Pine Ridge Reservation in South Dakota.

During World War II the Federal Government took the northern part of the Pine Ridge Reservation for use as a gunnery range. The Indians were promised that the land would be returned. It has not been, although the Defense Department declared it surplus in 1964. The National Park Service wants a substantial portion of this land to extend the Badlands National Monument.

The Indians of the Quechan Reservation on the California-Nevada border also have recently lost out to the "public good." For the past 75 years, these Indians, whose per capita income is less than $600, have been fighting for the return of a parcel of land that includes three miles of prime riverfront property. Although title to the land remained clouded (a decision on the case was pending before the Indian Claims Commission), the Interior Department in August 1968 decided to go ahead and lease the land to Yuma County, Arizona for 50 years. Non-Indian interests wanted the land as part of a park that will include a beach, hotel, zoo, and other recreation facilities.

In the name of progress and good neighborliness, the BIA grants rights-of-way across Indian land with little or no compensation to the Indian owner, for roads, pipelines and cattle. In one case, the Bureau granted a right-of-way for a 53,000-acre reservoir. The BIA has tried to change the rules so that the Indian owner need not give his consent.

Closely related to the taking of Indian land for the public good is the practice of relieving him of his land for what is termed "His Own Good." The phrase has an ominous ring to the Indian. It was for the Indian's "Own Good" that Congress enacted the allotment program, dividing tribal lands which were collectively owned, and distributing them piecemeal to the individual Indians. The Indians lost over half their land as a result. These are some of the ways.

Qualifying for welfare: The BIA, which has the legal power to determine the nature and availability of an Indian's assets, permits some states to treat allotted Indian trust land as a disposable and "available resource" even though the Indian himself cannot sell or mortgage his trust property and even though that property is exempt from taxation. Many states stipulate that one may not qualify for welfare if he holds such assets. The BIA helps the impoverished Indian qualify for welfare by allowing him to sell the land. Once the land is sold, the Indian still cannot qualify because he has the money from the sale of the land. He must spend the proceeds first—but only in a manner acceptable to the BIA. The BIA holds the money, and usually doles it out in installments equal to what the Indian would receive on welfare—generally less than needed for subsistence.

Partitioning land: Realty officers of the BIA can determine when a tract of land owned by several persons is partitionable. A non-Indian will acquire an interest in Indian land—especially if it is valuable crop or grazing land—and then seek a settlement with the Indian owners. He often can persuade the BIA to rule that the land may not be divided; he therefore is permitted to buy out the interests of the Indians in the entire tract of land.

Invalidation of wills: The BIA realty officer can thwart the Indian's wishes to will his land to whomever he wants—first, through his power to determine whether it is "efficient" for the land to be divided, and secondly, through his power to affect the Bureau's determination of the validity of the will.

The BIA can rule that a deceased Indian was incompetent in drawing his will, or that the will failed to make "adequate provision" for all the heirs. The Bureau refuses to define, or even provide guidance for, what constitutes "adequate provision." Such rulings nullify the will and the land is often sold to the highest bidder—usually a non-Indian.

Forced sales and manipulation: An Indian must secure permission from the BIA to sell his trust land. Often, permission comes with strings attached—requiring that the land be sold at public auction to the highest bidder, although the seller might prefer to sell to his tribe or to another Indian. Sometimes permission is conditional upon the immediate sale to a specific person, chosen by a BIA agent.

By establishing limitations on the way an Indian can use his land—for example, by establishing grazing limits and other "conservation" regulations—the Bureau makes it impossible for the Indian to make a living from his land. He is forced to sell or lease it.

Appointment of conservators: When the Indian is ruled "incompetent," a conservator is chosen to handle his property. In 1959, 27,000 acres owned by the Agua Caliente Indians of California was divided up in individual allotments to members of the tribe, but the land continued to be held in trust by the Bureau. The BIA's trustee responsibility, however, was shifted to state courts, and while the BIA paid little attention, court-appointed trustees pocketed much of the income from the land. After nine years of complaints by the Indians, an Interior Department task force investigated and found that guardians and conservators' fees had drained, on the average, more than a third of the ordinary income of these properties; that fees awarded by a judge in the case totaled as much as 340 per cent of total receipts from the land; that prime land had been left undeveloped; and that parcels of land had been sold by the trustees, without the Indians' consent.

Land as Sustenance and Income

Integral to the Indian's understanding and need for land is his understanding of survival. The right to hunt and fish, and work the land—these are inextricably intertwined with the Indian's whole makeup. In that light, the white man's assault on the Indian's right to exploit his land, and earn from it, is an attack upon the Indian himself.

LAND AS SUSTENANCE

The land yielded sustenance before it yielded money. And the Indian recognized long ago that the right to draw sustenance from the land was synonymous with what later immigrants to these shores called the inalienable right to life itself. The Indian has clung to his right to fish, hunt, and harvest wild rice even more tenaciously than he has to the land itself. To the Indian the right to hunt and fish are more than a right to eat—they are essential aspects of a religiously ordained pattern of existence which unites man and nature:

"On the Quinault River my people [went out] when the first sockeye [salmon] first entered the river along about the first of December, and this fish was taken. And this fish was cut lengthwise into strips, and there was a feed. There was a celebration and an offering to the gods of nature for the return of the fish because our people respected nature to the point of worship. And the bones of these fish which were not cut were placed back into the river as an offering. When we first started talking of a commercial fishery, my people were afraid to sell fish to the white man because they thought, well, they are going to cut the fish crosswise, and they will destroy the fish run. The fish won't come back, and little did they know how accurate they were." [1]

The economic, religious and ethnic centrality of hunting and fishing is formally acknowledged and protected in treaty after treaty. It has been recognized by the courts and given special status by Congress in recent laws. As the supply of wildlife has dwindled and the demands upon this supply grown, conflict has arisen between the Indian's right to sustenance and the sports and commercial fishing interests.

Nowhere has the conflict risen to a more symbolic or more violent level than in the fishing rights controversy in the State of Washington.

On the evening of October 13, 1965, about 100 Washington State troopers and game wardens, supported by a flotilla of boats of all sizes, staged a paramilitary raid on an obscure waterfront spot called Frank's Landing on the Columbia River. It was one of several sorties in a campaign against the Indians during which state forces teargassed, black-jacked and otherwise subdued some two dozen Indians—men, women and children ranging in age from four to 80 years—fishing there. Troopers smashed the Indians' canoes, scuttled and confiscated their tackle, slashed their nets and went about their business in a brutal fashion, enforcing state laws prohibiting the use of set nets and forbidding fishing out of season.

This was the climax of a series of clashes between state authorities and Indians of a dozen northwestern tribes—Quileutes, Puyallup, Nisqually, Muckleshoot and others—extending back some 15 years and continuing to flare up today.

> "Natural salmon propagation requires a delicate balance of conditions in streams and rivers. This balance has been upset and salmon production severely curtailed and in many cases destroyed, by the inevitable result of expanding civilization. For example, water pollution due to industrial waste and contamination, and due to urban sewage pollution, has contributed heavily to elimination of spawning grounds. As the demand for electric power increases and more dams are built, the result is further reduction of spawning grounds." [2]

The methods of intimidation are not subtle: discriminatory laws and rules, threats against fish buyers who deal with Indians, self-censorship to the point of a blackout by the local press and media, a stream of state propaganda aimed at stimulating prejudice against the Indians, harassment and confiscation of gear, and—in the courts—high bail, stiff penalties and little or no available counsel for the Indian facing state charges.

The biggest fishing assault on the salmon each year comes from sportsmen, accounting for up to 77 per cent of the catch. Washington, Oregon and the other states are naturally reluctant to tamper with sports fishermen, who bring with them a sizable amount of tourism. On the contrary, everything is done to lure them. There are "fish ladders" at Bonneville Dam and at the other dams on the Columbia. At Mud Mountain Dam on the White River, the fish are trapped and carried on trucks around the dam. At the new Mayfield Dam on the Cowlitz River, a complex combination of ladders, elevators, and trucking is used.

"For some of the reaches high up in the Columbia, it
has cost us as taxpayers $2,000 per salmon to save them,
and that is very, very expensive." [3]

Nonetheless, it is the Indian, with his miniscule fish catch
who is singled out for special attack. Rationales advanced by
the state are many. They have the appearance of logic and
science, but they are spurious.

Eskimo salmon fisherman empties his net.   PAUL CONKLIN

THE STATE *versus* THE INDIAN

1. The Indian poses a special threat to the salmon. He fishes upstream. Every fish he catches is one of the few to have survived to return to spawn. With new nylon mesh nets, the Indian can catch all returning salmon and utterly annihilate an entire run of salmon which return cyclically to spawn only in that particular stream.

1. A fish is a fish is a fish —whether caught upstream, downstream or in open seas. The Indian takes in less than 10 per cent of all salmon caught. 91.4 per cent of the fish landings in the State of Washington are non-Indian. The Indian is unwilling to forfeit his treaty rights and forego his seven or eight per cent of all salmon caught until the state has proven that it cannot protect the salmon adequately by first restricting the fishing of others. For it is the vast growth of commercial and sports fishing plus dam construction that cause the problem.

2. The Indian is only being subjected to the same rules and regulations that everybody else is. Piecemeal control simply will not work. One cannot approach a total ecological problem with certain parts left unregulated. The existing situation results in partial regulations of the fishery, or, when particular Indian tribes exercise their regulatory authority, dual regulation of the same resource. This has made effective management difficult if not impossible and constitutes a serious threat to the continued maintenance of the salmon and steelhead resources.

2. Nowhere but *upstream* where Indians fish is the prohibition against set nets actually applicable. Downstream they are extensively used by commercial fisheries who also use radar and other devices to spot and detect entire schools of fish. By curious coincidence, the prohibition on set nets does not bother the sports fisherman who is only interested in using a line with bait and only interested in protecting those three species of salmon (Chinook, Silver and Pink which together with the steelhead or rainbow trout) are defined as game fish because they rise to a lure. Moreover, state and federal fish agencies do little or nothing to perpetuate the runs of salmon originating on Indian streams and rivers—in marked disparity to the vast expenditure made to protect and preserve runs of fish on other streams.

THE STATE *versus* THE INDIAN

3. These fish were paid for by others—by sportsmen's associations and not by taxpayers—in order to stock the streams with steelhead. Indians should not be permitted to take that which was paid for by others. Indians have used their special treaty rights to catch fish produced at the expense of others and released for public benefit.	3. By stocking streams with steelhead and paying the salaries of the game commission, sports interests have attempted to convert a resource upon which Indians rely for subsistence into a private pleasure area for game fishing only. Indians fish for subsistence, not for sport—and not for steelhead (though some get caught in their nets). The dollar that pays for stocking the river will never feed the Indian or recompense him for the right taken away.
4. Recent decreases in salmon runs can only be countered by appropriate regulatory action.	4. The decrease in salmon runs has not been shown to be caused solely, primarily, or even largely by Indians. The state opposes neutral studies by federal authorities which might affix blame fairly and find out the true facts.
5. Conservation of a unique natural resource requires total and highly technical management by a neutral governmental body possessed of special expertise.	5. The Game Department is hardly a neutral body; its purpose is to expropriate Indian rights and Indian rivers for sports fishermen. It is supported totally out of revenue from hunting and fishing licenses.
6. The public interest — of conservation, of competing commercial and sports fishermen, of the larger tourist economy of the state—requires that the right of a special few give way to the larger social good.	6. The sports fishermen do not want to pay the millions of dollars which Indians' rights have been found by courts to be worth in the past. Instead they prefer to use the regulatory power of the state to extinguish the Indians' rights so that there need be no such compensation. License fees, however expensive, are still cheaper than claims awards. Under the guise of regulation, what is really involved is a taking of the Indians' property, *allegedly* for a public purpose *without* just compensation.

If the Indian does not pose a significant threat to the survival of salmon, why does the state unleash the full force of its police powers against him?

First, the Indian provides a convenient scapegoat. There is intense prejudice against him locally; he is limited in his ability to fight back; he has few allies; injustice against the Indian goes largely unnoticed by non-Indians; and there is generally resentment against the Indian having any special rights no matter how dearly the Indian paid for those rights, or how precious those rights are.

Second, focusing the blame on the Indian distracts attention from the fundamental but more politically explosive causes of depletion in the salmon supply—the urban interests requiring sewerage and electric power, the commercial fishing corporations, the sports fishing and tourism industry which is crucial to the state's economy. Most state officials are simply unwilling to tackle all these powerful interests.

Third, by zeroing in on the Indian, the state agency can strengthen and serve its own interest, and gain new, powerful allies. Federal intervention can be circumvented by defining the problem as essentially a state matter. Sports fishing and tourism interests are naturally willing to join forces and support governmental assault on Indians that screens their own activities against the salmon. And the authority of state game and marine biology officials creeps into a far vaster area, extending their empire into regional planning, land management, economic development, Indian affairs and tourism.

The fishing rights controversy is symbolic of a pattern of attacks on Indian treaty rights which reserve to Indians the right to draw sustenance from the land—from fish, deer, squirrels and game birds to wild rice. The attitude of state officials remains constant. * It is summed up by one official, speaking at a public meeting on Indian fishing rights when he introduced himself, saying: "My name is Mike Johnson. I am Assistant Attorney General for the State of Washington, and I am on the side of the salmon and, therefore, on the side of justice." [4]

---

* The outcome of the conflict between these two conceptions still hangs in the balance. A decision, just rendered in the U.S. District

LAND AS INCOME

Indian land is a source of income, but mounting evidence indicates that it is the non-Indian who is the prime—and sometimes the sole—beneficiary of the revenue produced by Indian land.

Thus, on the Pine Ridge Reservation in South Dakota, second largest in the United States, Indians cultivate less than one per cent of their land. Non-Indians use more than half of the Reservation for their own purposes, reaping substantial profits. At the Fort Hall, Idaho Reservation the BIA reported in 1967 that there were 208 non-Indian farmers but no full-time Indian farmers. Less than one-third of the land was being used by Indians. Some Indian landowners received as rent less than one per cent of the net profit derived from use of their land—under leases negotiated and approved by the Bureau of Indian Affairs.

For the fiscal year ending June 30, 1967, according to the BIA, over $7.9 million dollars was paid in royalties to the Osage Nation. The Bureau failed to mention, however, that one-half of those who received these royalties were "Indians" with less than one-quarter Osage blood since membership in the tribe depends on ownership of mineral rights and not on degree of Osage blood. Mineral rights have passed out of Indian hands over the years, sometimes legally but often through fraud, coercion and even homicide.

The lease of property for a valuable, profit-making enterprise is expected to bring a substantial return to the lessor. To the Indian it brings little or no profit; in many instances the lessee exploits not just the land, but the Indians who own it as well. Prime examples are the trading posts on the reservation. Their leases must be approved by the BIA. They are

---

Court in Oregon, invalidated "conservation" regulations that ignored the treaty rights of Indians to a fair share of the fish, and divided up the entire fish catch of the Columbia River between sports fishermen and commercial fishermen.

The court stated: "There is no reason to believe that a ruling which grants the Indians their full treaty rights will affect the necessary escapement of fish in the least. The only effect will be that some of the fish now taken by sportsmen and commercial fishermen must be shared with the treaty Indians, as our forefathers promised over a hundred years ago."

a monopoly franchise created to serve a special market, the Indians' need for goods. Despite these checks and advantages, the trading posts hardly qualify as public service operations. Some of these "corner store-type" operations are said to gross up to $500,000 annually.

A recent study of reservation trading posts revealed exorbitant prices, outrageous pawnbroker lending and interest practices and credit and debt collection procedures which would not be tolerated off the reservation. A can of coffee which costs the trader on the Navajo reservation 75 cents is resold to the Indian for $2.85. An Indian boy who ran up a $4 bill at a post on a Navajo Reservation in the Southwest was confronted by the trading post operator, who demanded immediate payment. The youth said he could not pay, and he was beaten, knocked down, kicked and left bleeding.[5] A valuable silver and turquoise belt was pawned and the borrower was charged 10 per cent per month interest, although the BIA legal limit for interest is two per cent.

The trader is often both the postmaster and banker for isolated Indian villages. When Social Security, welfare or salary checks come in by mail, the trader simply applies them to the Indian's trading post account. The Indian never sees his check, except when he is asked to sign it. To refuse to hand over a check to the trader is unthinkable, because the trader is the sole source of the essentials necessary to survive.

In an effort to stop such practices the Navajo poverty program, the Office of Navajo Economic Opportunity at Fort Defiance, began distributing checks by hand. But ONEO supervisors had to request protection because of threats from traders. Employees seeking to cash paychecks at trading posts still find "deductions" made.

Sources on other reservations report that traders and local store owners require the Indian to sign a check on a bank where he has no account. Failure to pay promptly and patronize the store loyally results in arrest and conviction on *criminal* charges for signing a fraudulent check. The sheriff thus doubles as local collection agent—though imprisonment for debt is unconstitutional.

Because he is the only source of credit or supplies and is the sole market for Indian crafts and produce, the trader supposedly is subject to careful regulation by the BIA. That is rarely the case. Ted Mitchell, director of a legal services program for the four-state Navajo reservation, has charged that the Piñon Trading Post pays for goods—sheep products such as wool which the Indian sells—with a form of scrip or line of credit to be used only at that trading post.

A general store.   PAUL CONKLIN

". . . In most cases cash is refused to Indians for their produce," he said.

The Bureau has clear responsibility, written into federal regulations, ". . . to see that the prices charged by licensed traders are fair and reasonable," and that ". . . the quality of all articles kept on sale [are] good and merchantable." [6]

The BIA's Navajo Area Director, Graham Holmes, admitted recently that he has the power to control prices and quality at the trading posts, but said he didn't agree with that sort of role for government. Besides, he said, when the area urbanizes, competition will spring up and the problem will be solved. The area is wasteland—bare, bleak desert.

The Department of the Interior, acting as representative of the Indians' interests, negotiated a lease on valuable Wyoming acreage belonging to two tribes. Its terms brought Humble, Continental, Pan Am and Farmers Union oil companies an extra $11 million—but brought the Indians nothing. The arrangement was made without the Indians' consent. The oil companies sought to modify their existing contract to allow secondary recovery operations (water-flooding), providing an estimated five million barrels of oil. This required consolidation of leases with the four companies into a single lease, and also required a right-of-way over tribal land to pipe water from Wind River. The Indians—members of the Shoshone and Arapahoe Tribes at Wind River Reservation—sought compensation. The oil companies refused. The BIA sided with the companies. The companies won.

In another dealing with the petroleum industry, the same Indians were receiving royalty payments on gas leases which a private consultant told them were far too low. The Indians complained to the BIA, asking why the rates were low and why a spot check revealed the royalty rates varied under a single lease. The BIA went to the oil companies, Atlantic-Richfield and Shell, and accepted their offer to correct the irregularities and pay retroactive royalties only on the leases which were cited in the complaint as examples. The BIA went to the U.S. Geological Survey (also part of the Department of the Interior) with questions on the computing of royalty payments.

It took two years to get an answer, and the answer was that while USGS makes an occasional cursory check of royalty payments, it relies mainly on the companies to determine what should be paid. In substance, the companies were left to regulate themselves. The BIA still relies wholly on the Geological Survey in looking after Indian oil and gas interests, despite a GAO report documenting extensive incompetency, lax and inadequate inspection procedures and other weaknesses.

In 1962, the Navajos decided to surrender substantial water rights in the San Juan River, so that water could be diverted to towns and cities in New Mexico. In return, the Government promised the Navajos an extensive irrigation project to convert 110,630 acres of dry land into farm land. A single act of Congress authorized both the dam and the Indian irrigation project; but while the Navajo project is only 20 per cent complete and has been consistently underfunded, the San Juan-Chama project to benefit non-Indians in New Mexico is 50 per cent complete. Money has been no problem. Both projects are being constructed by the Bureau of Reclamation in the Department of the Interior. As Daniel M. Ogden, Jr., Director of the Budget Office of the Secretary of the Interior, testified:

> "These programs [the Navajo irrigation project] have been held to a minimum in order to help reduce the deficit and lessen inflationary pressures on the economy." [7]

Domestic spending cuts seem to apply only to Indians in this instance. Plans are in the works to reduce the size of the irrigation project substantially and push instead for use of the water for sanitation and drinking purposes as a "substitute."

For decades the Indian has asked, "How come you can do it for whites, but not for Indians?"

He has asked it of the BIA and the U.S. Department of Agriculture regarding Indian participation in farm subsidy programs. Few Indians participate in the USDA farm subsidy. Instead, Indian land is rented at nominal prices to white farmers who consolidate the acres with their own, and raise two crops to establish a "production record." The farmers then are paid by the U.S. Government many times what is paid the Indian owner to take this same land out of production and do nothing. Lawyers who have delved into the problem say the BIA could encourage Indian participation in the farm subsidy programs. It could help provide the

Wind erosion on the Utah Uintah and Ouray Reservation. **BIA**

farm equipment needed to establish a production record and use available techniques for land consolidation, while pushing for legislation to eliminate present barriers to consolidation.

The BIA could charge higher rents for Indian lands used by white farmers, enabling the Indian at least to share indirectly in the farm subsidy payments. Finally, the Department of Agriculture could, in the case of Indians, relax its requirements which place the Indians at an unfair disadvantage.

Today much Indian land lies useless—or is of negligible value—because of lack of initiative by the BIA to solve the so-called "checkerboard" and "heirship" problems. The problem is an old one—originating in the Allotment Act of 1887, when Congress took large tracts of tribal land and divided it into individual "homesteads" of 80 to 640 acres. The sale of individual allotments has resulted in a checkerboard pattern of ownership with Indian land divided by non-Indian land. The Bureau claims it cannot find a way under present law to consolidate these holdings for maximum benefit to the owners or the tribe.

Much Indian land remains idle because it has passed down undivided over the years to countless descendants of the original owner, and then to the heirs of heirs. At least six million acres of Indian land is in heirship status. Multiple ownership prevents development by Indians, keeps the value of the land down and makes it impractical to develop, lease or sell without the consent of the owners. An income loss to the Indians of $417,868 for the year 1958 alone was attributed to nonuse of lands resulting from heirship problems.[8] The BIA estimates it will take 10 years or more to computerize its land records so that it can cope with this problem.

The legal authority to solve both problems has rested with the Bureau of Indian Affairs since 1934 (with tribal consent). Certainly the Bureau has no difficulty working out arrangements with non-Indian lessors and buyers which enable them to consolidate scattered parcels of land or develop heirship land quite profitably. Urban renewal and redevelopment agencies deal routinely with "heirship" problems by placing money in trust until the owners can be established but the Bureau finds its hands tied—except when non-Indians are prepared to solve these problems at the expense of Indians.

The BIA, "in the best interest of the Indian," discourages competitive bidding, assuring the same low price for the Indian's land. The BIA realty officer for Fort Hall, Idaho defended his failure to advertise leases aggressively with proud statements of confidence in the 25 major non-Indian leaseholders with whom he deals: "We know what we've got in these lessees. They're great farmers. And anyway, the trend is to increasing the size of farms."[9]

The BIA encourages improvement leases. At Fort Hall, some non-Indian leaseholders receive what amounts to a 90 per cent discount on their rent by promising to install a well or irrigation system.[10] When the installation takes place, it usually is done with inferior equipment which deteriorates by the time the lease ends. Where standards are specified in the lease, the BIA does little to enforce them.

The Indian typically must rely on the BIA to appraise his property in order to set lease prices. The appraisals are slow and inefficient. John Dressler of the Fallon Reservation, in Nevada, complained, "the appraisers are inefficient and do not know the land of our area. They are known to have appraised lands by the fields next to the one in question. Because of the scattered alkali deposits in this area, this method is highly inaccurate. The appraisers do not use the soil samples and do not allow the owner to show his land. . . ." Similar complaints have been voiced regarding appraisals for timber and oil properties.

Trespassing by non-Indians causes substantial income loss to Indians whose land offers fishing, hunting or grazing resources. The BIA rarely enforces Indian trespass rights. Non-Indian sportsmen trespass to fish and hunt in the Kakagon Slough swamp area, on the Bad River Chippewa Reservation in Wisconsin. The economy of nearby Ashland is dependent upon trade brought by these illegal sportsmen. The BIA refuses to help keep them away. Emmett Riley, the BIA superintendent for the area, claims he has no funds to enforce trespass rights, and doubts that the BIA is responsible for enforcement. In Minnesota, a local resort operator dug a canal across land belonging to the Consolidated Chippewa tribe at Leech Lake. The BIA provided no assistance in prosecuting. Ranchers without leases often permit their cattle to roam on the Fort Berthold reservation in North Dakota. The BIA has refused to enforce trespass regulations.

It is an elementary and fundamental doctrine of property law that a land owner may secure a right of way or easement "by necessity" when his property is "landlocked" and he cannot get to it except by traveling across the property of another. This is law—for non-Indians. The BIA honors it.

When non-Indians need easements over Indians' lands, the BIA responds. Edison Hinman of the Ponca Tribe in Oklahoma says a county road was built over his land to give non-Indian farmers access to a country road. When he complained that he had not given permission, Hinman says, he was dropped from the commodity food distribution program.

However, when Indians require easements by necessity to get to their own land, the BIA takes a different view. A typical example of this happened in Osage County, Oklahoma. BIA Superintendent John L. Pappan has refused to seek easements for roads needed by the Osage Indians. The Osage pay taxes which are supposed to go back into the county for roads. Pappan disagrees with the tribe on the availability of the money, and on where the duty to build roads in the county lies. He refuses to pressure county officials, saying that, after all, County Commissioners "have to get elected;" building roads for Indians might not be particularly popular for a candidate. Similar complaints have been voiced by the Creek Indians near Henryetta, Oklahoma.

The BIA has been worse than sluggish about investigating new resources on Indian land. In 1962, a Stanford University study of the BIA Osage Agency called for a greater effort to "identify and exploit mineral reserves other than gas and oil." Four years later, a separate study cited the same deficiency and said it was limiting the development of Indian lands. In 1969, a White House paper on Indian problems commented generally that the BIA's resource surveys have been uneven in quality and usefulness.

The oil companies find the BIA's failure to explore for minerals together with the red-tape lease approval system to their liking. The companies make a deal with an Indian for previously undrilled property, and sign a lease to be approved by the BIA. While the BIA takes months reviewing the lease, the company drills nearby and attempts to determine if there is oil on the Indian's property. If they strike oil, they can get the property at the pre-discovery price; if they find no oil, they simply withdraw their offer which still awaits BIA processing. Either way, the Indian is the loser.

The BIA delays the payment of money legally due the Indians.

In many cases, the hardship of Indians is increased— and their inability to improve their lot permanently in the long term is insured—by the way in which the Bureau chooses to distribute lease payments. In some cases, the Indian must wait until the end of the lease period to receive any payment whatsoever. In other cases, lease payments are spread out, even though the Indian needs the money to improve his home or business.

In 1938, the BIA established $1,000 as the upper limit of a quarterly payment that a "restricted" Osage Indian (one not judged "competent" by BIA standards) could receive from leasing his mineral rights in Osage County, Oklahoma. That limit remains in force today. Income in excess of that $1,000 a quarter is declared surplus and held by the Trustee Service Branch of the BIA. To get the money the Indian must show that it is needed for health, education or productive purposes; there is an assumption that otherwise it might be squandered. The Indian is forced to beg for money that is already his.

Another manifestation is the "90-day authority" which belongs to BIA realty officers. It allows a parcel of Indian land to be leased without the consent of all the Indian owners. If, after 90 days, permission still is withheld, the BIA superintendent can set the terms and sign the lease on behalf of the owner—without his permission. Katie Bird of the Otoe community in Oklahoma reports that Indians have been forced to accept five-year leases in this way.

On the Turtle Mountain Reservation in North Dakota, several Indians report the leasing of their lands to oil and gas companies, without their consent.[11]

In Osage County, Oklahoma, an Indian discovered that her land had been leased for three years, only after she decided to move there. The BIA had never bothered to tell her, nor to collect the rent and pass it on to her.[12]

The BIA also permits "blank check" leases—in which potential leaseholders convince the Indian landowner to sign an agreement to sign a lease contract in which the specifics have not been included. The prospective leaseholder then fills in the blanks and the BIA enforces the lease provisions.[13]

Land is also the basis of the BIA's authority, as the

Indian's trustee. It is the foundation upon which all the Bureau's powers rest, and is the Indian's only hope and last vestige of his past and freedom. His trustee has failed him— failed to represent, protect, bargain for, monitor, rectify or perform any of the responsibilities which fall on a trustee. As sustenance and as income, the land continues shrinking.

The Economic Developer's Definition— Land as the Future

With the riches of America all around him, the Indian lives in the poverty of an underdeveloped nation. The Federal Government and the Bureau of Indian Affairs keep it that way.

Indians have the prime ingredients for economic development: land, capital and labor. The land potential is unlimited: agriculture or livestock development, industrial use, mineral exploitation. It could yield income, employment and self-sufficiency for the Indian.

Although most Indians remain poor, they do not lack for natural resources. They also have certain water rights—and in the West, water is gold—for drinking, hydroelectric power industrial development, reclamation, irrigation and farming.

Indians do not lack for potential capital. Indian trust funds—from mineral leases and from Indian Claims Commission awards—totalled over $330 million. But no way has been devised to use that money as a source of capital or a form of collateral to generate maximum economic return.

Indians certainly do not lack a supply of labor. Nearly half the adult male work force is unemployed and many more are underemployed or seasonal workers. Skill training, genuine job opportunity, managerial experience, and opportunities for entrepreneurship have been largely lacking.

The Indian lives in an underdeveloped country—the reservation. His poverty stems from an unfavorable balance of payments, forced upon him by imports he neither wants nor uses. The cash inflow resulting from the present level of government expenditures on Indians averages approximately $5,000 per family.[1] That money, however, does not stay on the reservation. It drains away since its recipients are primarily BIA employees. The millions of dollars spent for construction on the reservation flow into the hands of non-Indian contractors, who often employ Indians only in menial positions. The money received by individual Indian families from welfare benefits, production of handcraft, and such employment as is available on the reservation immediately flows off the reservation again. The conduit is the economy at the Trading Post, owned and operated (with BIA approval) by non-Indians.

The Indian is in effect required to "buy" schooling, roads, and governmental services from the U.S. Government. A substantial portion of those services are purchased with the Indian's own money—revenue received from leases, mineral exploitation and also claims awards which are deposited in a bank which often pays no interest or a minimal return of four per cent interest. The Indian is required to pay, today, for goods and services which were "given" his father and grandfather during the last century. Many land claim awards made to the Indians have been reduced by the estimated value of services which the Government rendered to the Indians in the past, a sort of retroactive taxation.

He cannot use his substantial trust funds, because the BIA prefers to dole them out in small installments. He cannot exact a fair return for the value of his lands—mineral rights, the use of his water, the division of water rightfully belonging to him or simple rentals—because he is not free to bargain for himself. His own bargaining agent is also the purchaser or agent for the purchaser. The BIA is subject to political pressure from local governments and private interests which covet Indian resources. The Indian cannot develop his own manpower supply because the only effective "on-the-job training" is located off the reservation. Urban relocation of the Indian has drained many of the best young Indians away.

If the Bureau were serious about providing self-sufficiency on the reservation for the Indian, it would adopt the underdeveloped country model: consolidate land holdings, assist in helping Indian society work out a balance between consumption and investment, block the outward flow of cash and invest trust funds more aggressively on behalf of the Indians. Instead, efforts at industrializing the reservation have been systematically thwarted by BIA actions and incompetency. Land has been rendered unusable or tied up in bureaucratic red tape; job opportunities and training have been created only off the reservation; and BIA policies and practices have barred access to capital for economic development. Private sources of money are reluctant to invest on Indian reservations, because the BIA has failed to clarify the legal status of businesses on Indian lands.

The BIA promotes its programs in the name of economic self-sufficiency for the Indian. The Allotment Act of 1887 divided and distributed tribal land among the Indians, attempting to remake them in the white man's image—a homesteader tilling the soil—a rugged individual. But its effect was to break up the tribes, fragment the land and make "surplus land available for white purchase and occupancy." By 1934, two-thirds of the land held by Indians at the time of the Allotment Act had passed into the hands of the white man.

The termination policy of the 1950's similarly sought to give the Indian self-sufficiency and create incentives for individual achievement. Instead, the Indian's land and wealth were taken by private enterprise through forced sales to meet state taxes. In little time many terminated Indian tribes were shattered, near-bankrupt, such as the once-prosperous tribes of Klamaths and the Menominees. The Menominees made a determined effort to keep going their one enterprise, a lumber company, but with little success. Now, some of them are on the welfare rolls.

The relocation program, which takes Indians to the cities, and on-the-job training programs of Indians carry forward policies of forced acculturation and involuntary contributions to the non-Indian economy. Indians are promised steady employment and beautiful housing. A majority of those who relocate to the cities ultimately return to their reservation because the training programs have provided only short term subsistence work, with inadequate training and no future possibility of permanent employment at a decent wage.

The BIA's present stress on economic development and job creation on the reservation seems a break with the past. It is seductively plausible, but is, in fact, a repackaging of the same old goals—further expropriation of Indian resources from the reservations, and forced acculturation.

To date, efforts at economic development have produced remarkably few jobs in return for the investments of energy and money. The rate of plant failures has been high; only small marginal businesses have been attracted to the reservation. There have been numerous instances where firms have gone out of business, leaving the tribe with a substantial loss of the initial investment made to attract the industry to the reservation.

> "Jobs created in 10 years by the expenditure of millions of dollars in tribal and federal funds to lure outside corporations onto the reservation totaled 1,800. That meant 180 new jobs each year. It would be another 240 years before Indian unemployment would be eliminated at that rate—if the population remained static." [2]

The obstacles to economic development on the reservation are obstacles only if the purpose of economic development is to expropriate and acculturate. They would not be obstacles if the sole purpose of the economic development were to achieve self-sufficiency by optimal use of those resources at hand.

Members of the Yankton Sioux at Greenwood, South Dakota, established an electronics factory in the church community hall on their reservation, 18 miles from a paved road. There was no time clock in the hall and no daily work schedule. The 25 Indian employees worked as they chose. The arrangement fit the Sioux work preferences, leaving them free to work around the clock on some days and attend ceremonial dances or hunt on others. The factory produced well, met production schedules and acquired a formidable reputation among the Midwest companies with which it contracted. But when the Indians asked for an $8,000 expansion loan they encountered difficulties. The money would have purchased equipment to create jobs for the Santee Sioux, who lived across the river and could commute to the factory, but the BIA said the loan was not "economically feasible." Instead, it proposed a $115,000 loan to build a large building, hire time and motion studies and build a paved road. The Indians turned them down and borrowed $8,000 from a church.[3]

Many plants promise to hire Indians in order to secure permission to build on the reservations, but they end up hiring few. A baby furniture company said it would hire 100 Navajos, but after a year employed only 10. A garment factory which promised jobs for 125 Pima women was, after 17 months operation, employing only seven. Many businesses provide little training for the Indians they hire, and so they have a high turnover rate.

What sometimes appear to be Indian-run businesses in fact are controlled by the BIA. In Alaska, for example, the Bureau has set up a network of cooperative village trading stores, the Alaska Native Industries Cooperative Association (ANICA). ANICA is officially independent and native-owned. In practice it is wholly controlled by the BIA Area Office in Juneau, which made the loan to get it started. The BIA handpicks the white managers who run ANICA's central office in Seattle. In a recent interview ANICA's former general manager, Winfield Irvin, admitted that he opposed an OEO plan to expand the coops. "We couldn't get mixed up with OEO," said Irvin, "because we wouldn't have control of it." He said he had refused Labor Department funds to train workers because he didn't want "three government auditors running in here every week."

Several store managers have complained that the ANICA central office will not let them purchase generators and begin selling electricity (90 per cent of the villages are without electricity). Irvin said "We have to be careful not to raise the native's standard of living without first raising his ability to support that standard. Anyway, I lived without electricity when I was a boy."

Tribal enterprises which will not submit to total control find themselves systematically blocked in attempting to secure capital, obtain BIA permission to make needed capital improvements, bid on contracts or operate as a normal profit-making venture. In 1967, the Leech Lake Band of Chippewa Indians in Minnesota discovered a forgotten economic development plan that had been drawn up by the Bureau in 1961, recommending development of a recreation area on one of the tribe's lakes. The Indians had the plan updated, got an initial commitment from the Economic Development Administration and, without saying anything about finding the report, went to the BIA for the necessary approval. The BIA called for a study. When told they had already made the study, BIA said it would have to be updated. Told that it already had been updated, BIA said the recreation area could be built, but that an access road could not be widened to accommodate trailers because to do so would be to infringe on the "rights" of the whites who had leased Indian owned land alongside the road. To this day, nothing has happened.

Indian industrial development programs thus become simply extensions of urban relocation programs. They provide marginal jobs under sweatshop conditions. Their goal is to make a profit for non-Indian owners, and to provide the BIA with a handful of examples with which to illustrate the success of its economic development endeavors.

The current emphasis on industrial development masks an implicit rejection of those forms of cooperative agricultural and commercial enterprises which can produce for the inhabitants of the reservation and thus hold genuine promise of making the reservation economy fully self-sufficient.

The Bureau no longer promotes agricultural development on the theory that Indians can't be farmers because they refused to submit to the individualistic mold that the Allotment Act tried to impose. Recent government policies that attempt to train Indians to use their own land reflect a

*Navajo woman giving bottle to her spring lambs. Because
the area is too dry, the Navajo depend on the flock from
sheep and goats for their livelihood. The flock was badly
depleted during a recent blizzard.*   PAUL CONKLIN

crippling bias: "An Indian cannot be trained to use the
land." [4] Former BIA Commissioner Glen Emmons asserted
in 1956 that it is only "a rather small minority of our
whole Indian population which has any real interest or
aptitude for making a living by agriculture."

On the Colorado River Reservation in Arizona, the BIA
tried to train Indian farmers, but apparently failed to
follow through. The Indians involved in the project had
been sheep herders and were to use 80-acre assignments for
farming. One Indian described the procedure: "The Bureau
planted alfalfa on these assignments, and our people had
nothing to do but cut it. They did this the first year, the
second year, and the third year, each year getting a smaller
crop. The fourth year the alfalfa did not come up, and our
people who had been sheep herders all their lives did not
know what to do. Most of them came back to the sheep
ranges." [5]

Despite the extraordinarily high prices charged at trading posts for food—due in part to the cost of importing it—and despite the abundant availability of fertile soil and water, the BIA has largely washed its hands of promoting cooperative agricultural undertakings on the reservation, which might enable Indians to feed themselves. It contracted out the job to the U. S. Department of Agriculture Extension Service—an organization often unfit to perform the task.

Although there is land and water, Indians still go hungry. There are trading posts which could be run by Indians, welfare checks to buy food, and even food stamp programs which could provide a guaranteed revenue to tribal grocery retailers.

Tourism could be the Indian's greatest available industry. The current BIA approach to promoting it operates to further expropriation of prime, scenic Indian land. The BIA approaches tourism on a trickle-down theory: if the Indian gives up his scenic land and historic sites, then the state's tourist industry will prosper. It is assumed that the Indians somehow will benefit from a booming tourist business.

The Indian in the Northwest knows that he is more likely to be the victim of the tourist fisherman than the beneficiary. The Indian is often a chief tourist attraction, but he shares little in the revenues from the visitors. While the Deep East Texas Development Association and nearby Chambers of Commerce distribute tons of literature urging tourists to visit and learn from the Alabama-Coushatta Indian reservation in the marshy pinelands near the Texas-Louisiana border, the same brochures encourage the tourist to spend his money at hotels and shops in Lufkin, Livingston and other nearby towns—not on the reservation.

The New Mexico State Park Commission estimates that tourism brings $500,000 a day to the state economy, or more than $180 million a year. An independent study, paid for by the State, showed that Indians are what attracts many tourists to New Mexico. However, the Indians serve merely as a come-on to the tourists, who deposit their dollars in non-Indian coffers. In 1965, New Mexico Indians realized only $132,400 as their year's income from visitor use of their lands and facilities.[6]

Similarly, exploitation rather than economic development seems to be the goal involved in the give-away of the spectacular Badlands of the Oglala Sioux part of the Pine Ridge Reservation. The BIA is exploring giving this spectacular Sioux property to the National Park Service to increase the tourist industry on the Pine Ridge Reservation. If such an arrangement transpires, the Indian should receive a share of the income as well as benefits in the development, management and maintenance of the park site.

The BIA's failure to assert and protect the Indian tribes' special water rights belies the Bureau's sincerity and good intentions in promoting economic self-sufficiency through development. Water rights are among the Indian's most valuable holdings. Properly protected, they allow the Indian an advantageous bargaining position in securing other resources needed for prosperity. Without the water rights, the Indian will never see even a semblance of genuine economic development.

One-third of the Indian's land is idle, largely for lack of irrigation or available water. Between the Indian's legal rights to water developed under the so-called Winters Doctrine and actual access to that water, stand powerful public and private interests.

The Winters Doctrine holds that when the Indians gave up land to the United States treaties, they retained rights to water from that land to irrigate land which they kept. The Solicitor of the Department of the Interior is charged with protecting that right for the Indians.

The Bureau of Reclamation of the Department of the Interior is engaged in dam building and irrigation projects which directly threaten Indian water rights. The Solicitor of the Department of the Interior is also charged with representing the interests of the Bureau of Reclamation. Because water is a property right, the Department of Justice is authorized to defend the Indian's title to land. But when the Indian claims that a Government seizure of his land has been made contrary to law, then the Department of Justice must represent the Government, against the Indian. The Indian's two defenders, the Department of Justice and the Solicitors Office of the Department of the Interior, thus are aligned against him, assuring that his rights will be ignored or compromised.

At the turn of the century, the Yakimas of Washington State irrigated thousands of acres, turning their acreage into agriculturally useful land. They used the water from Ahtanum Creek on the northern boundary of their reservation. In 1906, the Bureau of Reclamation undertook the Yakima Reclamation Project which diverted much of the water away from Yakima lands. It took 55 years of legal haggling for the Indians to reestablish their rights to the water.

The Yellowtail Dam and Reservoir in Montana's Crow Indian Reservation provides still another example of Indians finishing last against the Bureau of Reclamation. There the Bureau not only did not pay the Crow Indians for their rights to water from the Bighorn River, but is selling the Indian water, depositing the proceeds to a non-Indian account and seeking to charge coal developers on the reservation for Indian water. The effect is to reduce the price of coal and decrease the proceeds to which the Indians are entitled.

The Soboba Reservation, near Indio, California, once had a thriving orchard, with beautiful trees and lush fruit. In the early 1900's the Los Angeles metropolitan water district drove a tunnel through a mountain near Soboba to carry water west to the parched new city. Soboba has been a desert ever since. With abundance turned to famine, the group splintered. Quarrels over allotments and assignment intensified. Now, 60 years later, the BIA is discussing with Soboba the substitution of an artificial irrigation system. The Indians are warned, however, that money expended for the system will be cut out of their future claims, and the Indians will have to pay for the water.

Talk about bold new programs and the promise to seek substantial appropriations for industrial development becomes meaningless when the BIA fails to protect the Indian water rights, thus giving away such an invaluable and indispensable resource.

Land as a Resource

"It is ironical that today the conservation movement finds itself turning back to ancient Indian land ideas, to the Indian understanding that we are not outside nature, but of it."   —Stewart Udall [1]

In a territory later called Nevada, a tribe of Indians—the Paiutes—owned a lake. The name was Pyramid Lake.

It was beautiful—much larger and more scenic than its famous neighbor, Lake Tahoe. Captain John Fremont "discovered" it "set like a gem in the mountains" in 1844, when the waters and banks were prosperous with fish and wildlife. Anaho Island off the northern shore served as a pelican rookery. Geysers, hot springs and rare oolitic sands were nearby, and the last of a species of prehistoric fish, the *Cui-ui,* swam unmolested.

Pyramid Lake was deeded to the Paiutes, a conquered people, in 1859. The white man had no need for the lake, and the land around it appeared worthless.

Today, Pyramid Lake is in danger of disappearing from the earth. The Paiutes are fighting both for its survival and their own.

The trouble began innocently enough. Control over Indian affairs shifted from the War Department to the Department of the Interior in 1859. In the early 1900's a new philosophy of conservation became Governmental policy. Interior was charged with special responsibility for conserving our country's precious natural resources and its scenic wonders. In the name of conservation, strange things started to happen. But they did not become visible immediately.

Irrigation was gaining use in the Western U.S. during the same period, and in the early 1900's, Interior dammed the Truckee River just above Pyramid Lake to divert water for the Newlands irrigation project. It was supposed to make cultivable some 287,000 dry acres, but in 65 years it has accomplished only a fourth of that—and the acreage proved to be inferior for farming and ranching. It takes twice as much water as is legally permissible to serve the land, largely because the irrigation ditches are unlined and 65 per cent of the water leaks out or seeps away.

Around 1930, the Indians found there were no more trout in Pyramid Lake. Water from the river had been diverted so that trout no longer could swim upstream to spawn. The tribe began legal efforts to regain the water, which had been diverted or appropriated without consultation. A few BIA officials sympathized and tried to assist the Paiutes but were fired or "promoted" away from Nevada.

The Indians fought alone for the most part, circumventing roadblocks the BIA and the Interior Department threw up and even winning a few minor court battles. Today, however, Derby Dam continues to divert more water from the river than can be used—even with the high percentage of loss. Some of the surplus is stored in a reservoir, some drains into Carson sink to evaporate, and some goes to a duck hunting preserve. Ranchers in the area use the preserve as a community cow pasture, and efforts to change things have been characterized as "a matter of cattle and ducks versus the need of the Paiute Indians." [2]

The lake sinks steadily, one to two feet a year. With it sinks the Paiutes' last hopes.

Interior's solution to the problem has been to propose still more dams. The Indians, not surprisingy, have resisted. They blocked the Washoe Project in 1963 and again in 1964. To win Indian support, Interior finally submitted a more acceptable plan, including these written promises to the Indians:

—The new dams would divert water from the Carson River, freeing water from the Truckee which feeds Pyramid Lake. More water would be available.

—New controls would be enforced on diversion, cutting waste and making still more water available for Pyramid Lake.

—No new dams could be built unless the survival of Pyramid Lake was assured.

However, Stampede Dam is half built and Pyramid Lake continues to shrink. In October 1967 the Interior Department altered its rules to liberalize the amount of water which could be diverted to the Newlands project. The additional water which was to come from Carson River never arrived. The Indians believe they were tricked.

A new threat, if it comes to fruition, will spell final doom for Pyramid Lake: a proposed compact between California and Nevada which will eventually take all the remaining water, leaving Pyramid Lake dry. The New York Times said the compact would give California rights to 50,000 acre-feet of water annually, with a right to use more as the need arises. "Thus as California puts more demands on the river, the level of Pyramid Lake will decrease even more rapidly." [3]

Roland Westergard, a Nevada state engineer who supports the compact, says Indians have no legal right to Truckee River water, although it is the only river feeding their lake. "There is not enough water to go around," Westergard said.[4]

Secretary of the Interior Walter Hickel took a firm stand. On March 19, 1969, he declared his opposition to the compact, stating that, "It threatens the survival of the 107,000-acre Pyramid Lake in Nevada, about 30 miles from Reno, and impinges upon the water rights of the Pyramid Lake tribe of Paiute Indians who own the lake." Hickel's support for the Paiutes and his opposition to the compact lasted four months. He has now agreed to a "compromise" that will drop the level of the lake almost 50 per cent. Even the Paiutes, by now surely accustomed to political treachery, were astonished. In July, James Vidovich, chairman of the tribal council, stated in anger and shock,

> "The Secretary told our tribal council that he would protect Pyramid Lake because it was a great national resource and he said he would not let anybody steal our water. We cannot believe the Department of Interior has adopted the absurd proposal. . .to drain our lake." [5]

At one time, the compact could well have been blocked

in Congress, but with Hickel's compromise the destruction of Pyramid Lake can be accomplished solely by administrative action. Hydrologists say that at the rate of present and planned diversions, Pyramid Lake could last but 100 years. Hickel has advanced the timetable.

The Indian understands that his worst enemies can be his seemingly well-meaning friends and protectors, who lull him with assurances and promises into a false and fatal sense of security. An example is the consistent refusal by former Secretary Udall to assert—as a matter of Department policy and as legal entitlement—the right of the Paiute Indians to water from the Truckee River for Pyramid Lake. Yet the Indians' claim has clear legal merit. The Department of the Interior has declined to assert in court the claim of the Indians to preserve their lake—or even to espouse the claim as the cornerstone of Departmental policy. Rather it has taken the position that the Indian should trust its good intentions and assurances of largesse.

Behind this refusal was always a thinly veiled threat that should the Indian press his assertion of right he would forfeit the good will of the Department and make it difficult for the Department to support him.

Pyramid Lake is not an isolated instance of the failure of the Department of the Interior to use its expertise and fulfill its conservation mandate on behalf of the Indian. It has failed the Indian equally with respect to all areas where its supposed capability and official responsibility are most specific: soil erosion, reforestation, grazing, water supplies, restocking of fisheries—and prudent management and development of land resources. The role of management and conservation of Indian resources has been an integral part of the pattern of dependency—where the Indian pays the white man to manage and exploit Indian resources.

Dams Kinzua Dam in Pennsylvania, creating Lake Perfidy in New York, is our nation's own special trophy of shame—for here, we broke George Washington's promise to the Senecas never to claim their land "nor disturb the Seneca nation." The promise was guaranteed in a treaty signed in 1794 and reaffirmed many times since. The Senecas were flooded out.

Timber Reforestation regulations go unenforced. Timber interests played a significant role in securing the termination of treaty rights of the Klamath Indians in Oregon; the same interests have played an intermittant role in blocking the path of the Taos Pueblo in securing possession of their New Mexico Blue Lake holy lands, and are bringing pressure for the termination of the Colville Indians in Washington. The forestry branch of the BIA manages Indian timber land. It charges the Indians 10 per cent of the gross receipts from the forests for administrative costs, a charge which usually exceeds actual cost of administration. The revenue is credited

Taos Pueblo. PATRICIA ALLOTT

to the Bureau's general accounts; it is not plowed back into improving forests or providing training programs for Indians.

The BIA's land management programs produce jobs for non-Indians, but neither income nor conservation training for Indians. At present, income from land management of the Indian timber land is delegated to the forestry branch of the BIA. Indians are hired solely in a labor capacity. No programs have been instituted to provide forestry and management training. High officials attempt to justify this practice, saying that it is more efficient to hire "experts." While not opposed to the idea of training Indians in forestry, the BIA has been unwilling or unable to undertake such a program which might bring conflict with the Agriculture Department's politically powerful National Forest Service.

The Indian knows all this. He wonders why it is so.

> *The frog does not*
> *Drink up*
> *The pond in which*
> *He lives* —An Indian Proverb

The Holy Man's Definition— Land as Sacred

> *Is not the sky a father and the earth a mother and are not all living things, with feet and wings or roots their children?* [1]

The American mind is capable of grasping the notion of a holy land in Jerusalem, Mecca, the Vatican—but not northern New Mexico.

To the Taos Pueblo Indians of New Mexico, the Blue Lake area is holy land. In resisting efforts by the United States Government since 1906 to expropriate the area, the Indians have stood by five principles. They are principles which the Federal Government finds unacceptable, but they nevertheless are the heart of the Indian's understanding of land—especially holy land.

HOLY LAND IS NOT FOR SALE. Despite their poverty, the Taos Pueblo Indians have continually rejected *generous* claims awards made to them by the Government. They desire only to reclaim their land, the sacred Blue Lake area. In 1926, the Indians went before the Pueblo Lands Board and offered to forfeit some $300,000 owed them for land within the town of Taos, New Mexico. All they asked was that the Board recommend the return of Blue Lake.

Thirty years later, the United States Indian Claims Commission confirmed their rights to 130,000 acres, including the 48,000 acres held as sacred. The Commission's cash settlement award was rejected by the tribe because it "cannot accept money for its sacred mountain land. Legally now, morally always, and in spirit which is outside of the time, this sacred land and its people have been joined together; they are one and the same."

HOLY LAND CANNOT BE DIVIDED. Congress seems incapable of comprehending this. Senator Clinton Anderson of New Mexico has repeatedly pressed the Indians to mark off those areas which are not sacred and has offered them, most recently, the exclusive use of 1,600 acres, which *he* views as the most sacred sites. He would divide the rest for public use. The Indians respond: all of this land is sacred, none more sacred than the other.

> "There are many shrines in this sacred area: Bear Lake, Deer Lake, Waterbird Lake and Star Lake, certain slopes where clay is dug and particular springs where plants are gathered for use in the ceremonies. But this area is not visited just for ceremonies, it is in constant use. It is a school where children are taught Nature and Indian lore, a place for family outings, and a source of berries, wood and herbs. It is their sanctuary, haven, school, storehouse and source."

> "Near the end of each summer, the people of the Pueblo travel back along the course of the Rio Pueblo to the sacred Blue Lake. This journey signified the return of the people to the source of their life and the source of their spirit. From the Lake to the Pueblo, the stream is the lifeline and the heartline of the tribe. For years beyond memory, the water, the land, and the people have been one interrelated and living whole." [2]

On September 19, 1968, Secretary Udall testified in favor of a bill which would have restored a 48,000-acre area to the Taos Pueblo Indians. His statement showed a rare understanding of how the Indians view Blue Lake—an understanding few others in the Government seem to share.

"Because of the essential secrecy of its religion," said a summary by Udall, "it has been difficult for the Pueblo to explain in terms satisfactory to the American mind why it must own and control the *entire* watershed of the Rio Pueblo [River]. . . . To insist that the Indians disclose more is to ask them to profane their holy mysteries. The watershed creates the Rio Pueblo de Taos. Blue Lake and numerous sacred springs are the sources of the stream. The waters of the Rio give life to the watershed and to the Indians who dwell therein; the Indians, in turn, give succour and husbandry to the watershed lands. Men and nature, in the watershed, are interlocked in an ecological and religious unity; preservation of the natural ecology of the area is as important to preservation of the religion as is the preservation of the Indians' religious privacy. Blue Lake, as the principal source of the Rio Pueblo, is symbolically the source of all life; it is the retreat also of souls after death, the home of the ancestors who likewise gave life to the people of today. The August ceremonies at Blue Lake serve to bind the youths of the Pueblo to the community as it exists and as it has existed over the centuries. Blue Lake, therefore, symbolizes the unity and continuity of the Pueblo; it is the central symbol of the Indians' religion as the cross is in Christianity. Because the symbolism of Blue Lake extends to the entire watershed, the entire area is sacred. The numerous shrines and holy places exist throughout the area because the watershed is sacred, the watershed is not made sacred by the presence of particular shrines. It would be a tragic misunderstanding to construe the Indians' religious use of the area as involving only occasional use of a few sacred precincts.

". . . Maintenance of complete privacy in, and the natural ecology of, the Blue Lake area are the most important factors in preserving the ancient religion. Domination of the Blue Lake area by tourists, campers, sportsmen and loggers will destroy both the privacy necessary for the practice of the religion and the natural ecology of the area which is an integral part of the religion in the lives of the people." [3]

In the face of this exhortation to set right a long-standing wrong, the Senate Committee offered the Indians a mere 3,150 acres to be held in trust by the BIA. In 1969, the offer was scaled down to 1,600 acres, to be set aside without fee title as a "religious area" for the Indians. The proposal was the work of Senator Anderson.

HOLY LAND IS NOT MERELY A RESOURCE FOR EXPLOITATION. It is not simply intolerance for the Indians' religious customs that has brought about the Blue Lake conflict. The area is rich with timber and potentially ripe for tourism. The National Forest Service, which is part of the United States Department of Agriculture, was charged with protecting the lands for the Indian over the past 30 years. In cooperation with the State of New Mexico, however, the Forest Service has allowed livestock to roam and over-graze the area, has issued a myriad of camping permits and has seriously considered entering into logging arrangements wth at least one lumber company. In cooperation with the State, the Forest Service has tampered with a sacred body of water, first by overstocking it with fish, then by dynamiting to kill the fish in order to maintain a balance of nature. In addition, Forest Service personnel have patrolled, taken pictures of, and intruded upon the privacy of religious ceremonies. It is their way of making sure, they explained, that the Indians were using their holy land in accordance with the Government's regulations and interpretations.

HOLY LAND REMAINS HOLY LAND WHILE A LIVING CULTURE SO DESIGNATES IT. The National Forest Service and several congressmen would require the Indians to show that each and every acre is being used for holy purposes. One of the chief rationales advanced for not giving the land in trust to the Indians was in order to guard against the possibility that they might lose their religious fervor and that their use of the land as a religious site might, over time, dissipate. Senator Anderson supports this line of reasoning. He has demanded that the Taos Pueblo Indians reveal all their secret religious rites and show that these rituals were being performed daily and continually in all parts of the area, and in effect to prove that the ceremonies warranted a special dispensation in connection with the Indians' land.

HOLY LAND REQUIRES A SPECIAL LEGAL STATUS—FULL TITLE HELD IN TRUST TO BE HON-

ORED ABOVE AND BEYOND NORMAL FORMS OF PROPERTY OWNERSHIP. The Taos Pueblo Indians have insisted on this with a peculiar tenacity. They are unwilling to settle merely for a perpetual right of exclusive use. To the analytical mind, there appears to be little difference. The Indian replies: if there is no difference to the white man, then why can he not give the Indian the land perpetually in trust? For the Indians, there is a difference, symbolic yet all-important. Even congressmen and the Forest Service know that they cannot treat land held in trust as lightly as they can a mere permit of exclusive use—even though in legal theory, they are the same. Having had long and painful experience with continuous abuse under an exclusive use permit provided by the National Forest Service, the Indians know that symbolism transcends legal analysis and therefore can determine the future as it has the past.

The conflict continues, and will continue, for the Government insists that the Indians weigh their sacred values against contemporary public needs and utilitarian standards. The Indians will not negotiate. "One Nation Under God" has its limitations, and the Indians' holy lands clearly fall outside them. Yet their vision persists and they have faith it will ultimately prevail.

> *"My friend, I am going to tell you the story of my life. . . . It is the story of all life that is holy and is good to tell, and of us two-leggeds sharing in it with the four-leggeds and the wings of the air and all green things; for these are children of one mother and their father is one Spirit. . .now that I can see it all as from a lonely hilltop, I know it was the story of a mighty vision given to a man too weak to use it; of a holy tree that should have flourished in a people's heart with flowers and singing birds, and now is withered; and of a people's dream that died in bloody snow.*
>
> *"But if the vision was true and mighty, as I know, it is true and mighty yet, for such things are of the spirit, and it is in the darkness of their eyes that men get lost. . . ."* [4]

THE BIA'S THREE LESSONS

In the areas covered thus far—land, education, and health—certain patterns have emerged. Where American Indians are concerned, virtually every activity of the Federal Government can best be understood as teaching one of three fundamental lessons—lessons that teach what kind of behavior will be permitted and rewarded, and what kind of behavior will be prohibited, frustrated or punished.

These three basic lessons hold true as the common denominators of Governmental practice and policy and proved the surest guides in attempting to unravel the complexity and seeming contradictions in the gray world which is Indian policy:

Lesson I. Self-realization is frustrated. It is futile and even dangerous to try to function on one's own terms in keeping with one's own culture, tradition and sense of identity.

Lesson II. Dependency is a virtue. To survive one must beg. Only incompetency and dependency bring rewards, gratification and security (to Indians on the reservations).

Lesson III. Alienation is rewarded. All the Indian must do to succeed is tear himself away from his land, his people and his heritage. Then—but only then—he can have economic security, prestige, power, approval and material wealth.

Lesson I: Self-Realization is Frustrated

It is futile and even dangerous to try to function on his own terms in keeping with his own culture, his people's tradition, and his sense of identity. This lesson has been taught by systematically destroying or withdrawing each of the

bases on which self-realization ultimately rests. *The roles or functions through which men normally express themselves and define their identities are denied to the Indian.* For example, the Indian male is faced with a choice of enforced idleness or leaving the reservation. "There are virtually no meaningful and socially rewarding roles for the Indian man," according to Dr. Gordon Macgregor, formerly a high-ranking BIA official. "He has become frustrated, anxious and listless. Without a career, he has lost his own self-respect and the esteem of his family and community. This has contributed to deep personal and group insecurity. Compared

Chicago storefront with sign reading "100 Women Needed." Peering out from behind the glass is an urban Indian. ED ECKSTEIN

with the excitement and virility of life in the past, the present existence has little meaning. . . . The loss of man's role as provider, husband and father thrusts the mother into the position of key family figure, which causes additional psychological and social difficulties." [1]

On many reservations the women are becoming the providers while the men look after the children. If the woman goes to work, the man is further demeaned. Father Justus Writh, a Catholic priest affiliated with a mission serving the Zuni reservation in New Mexico, stated the problem well: ". . . Many new industries are locating on our Indian reservations. . . . [But] the jobs are not going to our Indian men—to the fathers of families who really need the work. Instead the tendency is to give the jobs to women. . . . For our Indian mothers to be forced to take on outside work because there are no jobs available for men or because the jobs that are available are given to women is to fail our Indian people completely. . . . How much of a man would you feel if you wiped the running noses of your children and washed their diapers while the mother of your children went off to work each day so that she might feed you and buy your clothes?" [2]

Indian parents are regarded as incapable of properly raising their children. A 1965-66 Congressional report observed: "Since the majority of families in the Ponca tribal area are unaccustomed to modern living conveniences, a training program in "how to live" is essential. This program will need to be as elemental as how to flush a commode, how to wash hands, how to use an automatic stove, how to light a unit heater, and so forth." [3]

Indian college students are presumed equally uncivilized. The University of Kansas student newspaper reported recently: "During the student's second and final year at Haskell [a college for Indians in Kansas], he is taught social graces during specially-prepared meals in a campus dining room." [4]

The Indian cannot express himself through asserting his rights: he cannot even ascertain those rights. He is consigned to legal limbo.

"The American Indian has been referred to as *a people without law.* Perhaps it would be more accurate to say that the American Indian is a people with *too much* law. Not only are they bound by the laws governing other people in our country, but the Indian's legal rights are further complicated by a special body of law based upon more than 4,000 treaties and statutes and upon thousands of judicial decisions and administrative rulings. . . . The complexity and peculiarity of

Federal Indian laws have long baffled legal experts. As
for the average Indian, he has always lived in ignorance
of the laws governing him, and his ignorance has made
him a victim of despotism." [5]

Without lawyers and without recourse to protections
which other Americans take for granted, Indians are constantly subjected to theft, deceit, manipulation and intimidation. Yet their cultural survival as well as their basic rights
and traditions can only be protected against a world of hostile pressures if legal counsel is made available. As a California court recently declared, "In a mass society, which
presses at every point toward conformity, the protection of
a self-expression, however unique, of the individual and the
group becomes ever more important. The varying currents
of the subcultures that flow into the mainstream of our national life give it depth and beauty. We preserve a greater
value than an ancient tradition when we protect the rights
of the Indians who honestly practiced an old religion in
using peyote one night at a meeting in a desert hogan near
Needles, California." [6]

*The Indian is further stripped of the ability to assert
himself, by the absence of any effective administrative form
of review of his grievances or denial of rights.* If the Indian
fares poorly in the courts, it is worse yet in dealing with the
bureaucracy which controls his life. There he has no recourse or appeal. He is a ward and a supplicant. He is help-
less.

Like certain juvenile court judges who feel it is not in
the "best interests of a child" to provide due process, the Bureau of Indian Affairs can become highly offended when lawyers dare to tread into the benign system of care which it
administers. The Bureau believes that the interests of its Indians are best served without "outside meddling" by attorneys. Thus, most BIA rulings and judgments are final, with
no effective provision for appeal. Even when there is that
provision, the fact is that few rulings are questioned because, lacking knowledge or counsel, the Indian must simply passively accept the decisions of his keepers. Recently in

Oklahoma, a Bureau official secured a ruling that one of his charges, an Indian woman, was incompetent. That settled, he made her property entirely subject to control by a person designated by the Bureau. All this was done without the woman even being present. She found an attorney, contested the case and won a reversal.[7] Most Indians are not so lucky.

In the absence of legitimate appeal routes, the Indian's only recourse is to "come to Washington," where once in a while he can create enough waves in the office of a congressman or at the BIA to win his point. That is not what is normally meant, however, by an orderly, equitable and effective review procedure.

The Indian cannot control his own property or manage his own private affairs without continuously securing the consent and approval of the Bureau of Indian Affairs.

He is not even allowed to die "competently." Posthumously, his will is examined in great detail by Bureau officials. If, in the opinion of the reviewing official, the Indian has not done right by his relatives, the will is voided. The Government compounds the problem by refusing to issue guidelines on what constitutes adequate protection of relatives or to discuss the validity of a will during the period after it is drawn and before the Indian dies.[8]

Indians are not even allowed to use their own land for whatever purpose they choose unless they secure a permit issued after elaborate review by both the tribal council and the Bureau. Instances have been documented where this processing extended over six years.[9] But while the Bureau is careful to protect the Indian's land from the Indian, it is not protected from anyone else. Hunting and fishing rights on the Indian's land are still subject to discriminatory regulation by the states.

In sum, the Indian cannot use what is his—money, land, or treaty rights—without first securing approval. Individual Indians constantly report they cannot even find out what land is theirs, or what money is in their own private accounts. They cannot claim their basic rights as tribal members in some instances, because the Bureau will not tell them whether their names are still on tribal rolls. The rule seems to be: strip the Indian of all knowledge of who he is, what he owns, what rights he has—deprive him of ability to control his property, play a useful role, assert his rights, control his destiny.

Tribal governments fare no better. They, too, are denied information on their money, which is controlled by the Bureau through trust accounts. They are denied access to the money awarded them for land wrongfully taken in the past century. As a result, two-thirds of those claims awards still sit in U.S. Treasury coffers, undistributed. The tribes are unable to contest automatic deductions which the Government makes from the claims awards, a retroactive tax bite for services rendered in the past 100 years. Many tribes are still waiting their turn in line just to present their claims. The Indian Claims Commission, a special judicial body set up during the Truman Administration to settle fairly the Government's debts to Indians, is scheduled to expire in 1972, but after 23 years of operation it has processed only a fraction of the claims which Indians have filed.

Despite regular, periodic upbraiding by the General Accounting Office, the Bureau still handles the $330 million of Indian monies in its trust accounts with little regard for their earning potential. Until recently the funds lay fallow in the Treasury. Now, at GAO's insistence, the Bureau has permitted some tribes to invest their money in certain approved Government securities and bank deposit certificates. But a large portion of these funds remain in the Treasury, earning a modest four per cent interest, while some Indians receive no interest at all. The Indian has no choice: he is not free to invest his money elsewhere.

The Indian's capacity for self-realization is further undermined by denial of any degree of certainty regarding the present and the future. Planning is rendered futile by the Bureau's uncanny ability to keep the Indian off balance. He lives on sufferance from day to day. As William Carmack, director of the National Council on Indian Opportunity has said, "The United States has never been able to follow any

Indian policy with consistency—[not] even the policy of extermination."

Roy McIntyre, tribal council chairman of the Umatilla Tribe of Oregon, remarked that the "only promise the BIA ever kept with us is that it will always be our boss."

The examples are too numerous to be catalogued. Indians at a BIA regional conference in Las Vegas recently told Commissioner Robert Bennett: "In the past, many agricultural, recreational, timber and housing developments were started; and before the ink was dry and before any of the programs got off the ground, they were sharply curtailed or obliterated."

A Papago girl, Grace Cahora, can say from individual experience what it means to rely on the BIA. The day before she was to leave for college, her suitcase packed and her school acceptance in hand, the 18-year-old girl was told she could not go. No scholarship.

"I filed my application early . . . and I was given to understand there'd be plenty of money for scholarships," the girl said. "So when no word came . . . I just naturally thought that the money would come this week—right before school started."

The BIA administrator who handled her application admitted, "We probably were a little remiss in not letting her know that her application had not been processed" before scholarship funds were exhausted. Grace's college career was, he said, "sort of lost in the shuffle, but that's the way the ball bounces."

In defense, the administrator asserted, "The trouble with these Indian kids is the fact they don't get off their duffs and follow through on these things. Maybe if a few more like Grace get singed, the word will get around. . . ." [10]

Even where tribes theoretically have a representative form of government the BIA is omnipresent.

Mary Cornelius, a member of the Turtle Mountain Chippewa Tribe in North Dakota, reports that "when any officials have been elected by the tribal members there's always been a lot of interference by the Bureau of Indian Affairs. . . ." Mrs. Cornelius should know. In two elections for the tribal council, in 1966 and 1968, she received the most popular votes and was therefore entitled to the chairmanship. Despite these clear expressions of the tribe's will, Mrs. Cornelius, who is unpopular with the local Bureau agency because of her insistence that all of the Bureau's decisions which affect the tribe should be reviewed by the tribe, was denied the chairmanship and even a seat on the council as a result of certain actions of questionable legality by other members of the council. Pressure by the Bureau on the other members played a significant role in these episodes.[11]

At the tribal level, Indians are denied most of the options which the governed should hold. At the national level, they are denied them all. It is taken for granted that Indians will have no say in the selection of the Commissioner of Indian Affairs, who is appointed by the President to head the BIA and thus is viewed by Indians as the all-powerful federal official in their lives and destinies. In the enlightened 20th century, no Indian had ever been appointed commissioner until President Johnson selected Robert Bennett in 1966.

Local BIA superintendents are, as a rule, selected without consultation or concern for the wishes of the tribes they will supervise. At times when these superintendents generate great hostility and controversy on the job, they are removed by the BIA. Removal, however, invariably takes the form of transfer to another post, sometimes even a promotion, where other unsuspecting tribes must endure the official.

When the tribal chairman of the Pyramid Lake Indians dared to criticize the BIA, the superintendent of the Nevada Indian Agency told him "to recant" or "resign." He resigned under pressure. The tribe made enough noise to gain attention from Washington and the superintendent was removed from his position. It was hardly a victory, however. The superintendent was officially cited "for outstanding performance with the 26 tribal groups throughout Nevada," and promoted to a new post which—as the BIA press release proudly proclaimed—"will place under his administrative purview nearly all the Indian tribes of Washington, Oregon and Idaho." [12]

Indians have no real opportunity to shape their own tribal governments; the governments, and changes within them, are usually external creatures, often imposed against the will of the Indians. Once imposed, they persist despite opposition. In 1935 members of the Hopi Tribe were asked if they wished to take advantage of the newly passed Reorganization Act, which provided for the establishment of a tribal government with certain specified powers. The chief of the village of Shongopovi, Chief Keewanymuna, says his people discussed reorganization but decided against it. The BIA superintendent announced, however, that reorganization had carried. Shortly thereafter he called a second election to choose a tribal council which, under the Reorganization Act, would become the officially recognized Hopi governing body. The Hopi had always looked to the hereditary chiefs of their villages for both secular and religious leadership, and so they ignored the election. The superintendent, however, would not be stopped. He selected a handful of the Hopi whom he deemed "progressive" and installed them in office. The Hopi have been divided since, with a substantial number of villages continuing to follow their traditional leaders. Elections still draw only minimal participation, and in some villages virtually every member of the tribe abstains from voting.

The Chemehuevi Tribe in California found, as have other Indians, that even when they attempt to form a tribal government acceptable to the BIA, they meet frustration. The Chemehuevis finally were forced to hire a lawyer and threaten legal action after the BIA told them their constitution and by-laws, ratified on June 8, 1968, were unacceptable. "The BIA didn't tell us what was wrong with it, and what kind of words have to be used to be approved," tribal leaders said.[13]

The tribal council which governs the Osage tribe in Oklahoma is legally and effectively the board of directors of the Osage mineral estate, not representative of the Osage people. The council is elected by "shareholders"—people who hold rights in the mineral estate—at least half of which are of less than one-fourth Osage blood; six of the eight voting members on the council are of less than one-eighth Osage blood. Many of the voting shareholders live far from Osage County and are interested only in receiving their quarterly checks, not in the well-being of the Osage people. The problems of the Osage—unemployment, poor housing, welfare—go unattended. Many of the authentic Osage Indians have no voice whatever in council affairs since they hold no rights in the mineral estate. When the council speaks, it speaks for the shareholders of the mineral estate; it does not and cannot speak for the members of the tribe, yet this is what it purports to do.

What the Bureau wants, of course, are tribal governments in form, not in substance. The BIA model constitution, distributed at the time of the Reorganization Act to all tribes, requires that almost all tribal governmental actions be reviewed and approved by the Secretary of the Interior.

Acts of Congress are another means of imposing alien government on the Indians. With the passage of Public Law 280, a state gained the power to extend its jurisdiction and laws over Indian tribes without their consent. Only in 1968 was a provision made requiring tribal consent to state jurisdiction. Similarly, termination legislation has in the past unilaterally repudiated the Indians' special treaty rights and incorporated reservations by fiat into state and local government units.

Even the freedom to "go it alone," to engage in self-help projects, to band together to seek some common goal or secure outside help and assistance is withheld from the Indian. Tribal governments are discouraged and blocked from seeking outside help. They face deliberate delay, insuperable administrative obstacles and a threat of retaliation by the Bureau. In the face of concerted opposition by superior forces, few will undertake to create and build when the odds against success are so great. A tribe must have BIA approval to secure the services of a lawyer, an engineer, an architect or other professional help. Not surprisingly, if the Bureau opposes the project it can effectively block it. Thus, when the Papago Tribe in Arizona became impatient with the mediocrity of "experts" provided by the BIA, they sought to hire their own consultants at their own expense. The BIA threatened the tribe with total withdrawal of all BIA services.

In Minnesota, the Leech Lake Indians went to the U.S. Department of Housing and Urban Development (HUD) and obtained money to finance housing for the tribe. Unfortunately, HUD routed the funds through the BIA. The Bureau withheld them and set impossible conditions for release of the funds.

Ultimately, self-realization requires the power to shape one's future, to control one's destiny, to choose from a variety of alternatives. The Indian has no such power, no control and no choice.

Navajo outside a trading post, just off the reservation—thus liquor for sale.   PAUL CONKLIN

Lesson II: Dependency is a Virtue

To survive, the Indian must beg. All immediate reward, gratification and security on the reservation depend upon the Indian's consistent posture of incompetence and dependency. The Bureau of Indian Affairs has forged a tacit progress-without-progress arrangement with the Indians. It is a hoax, perpetrated by an agency which spends each day hedging against the next, while its charges do what they can to get by. For the Indians, the desirability and the need to remain dependent and incompetent is woven deeply into every facet of their daily experience and their history.

The Indian must remain incompetent and he must show that incompetency each day, if he is to continue to receive the assistance and the services which the United States Government provides. Every Indian tribe is keenly aware that if it attains a degree of economic and political self-sufficiency, it is in imminent danger of losing federal assistance, subsidies and access to federal intervention. Those tribes singled out for termination of all federal benefits were judged by the BIA to have attained a high degree of competency. Gary Orfield, in his study of the termination of the Menominee Indians, noted: "As the '50's began, the Menominee tribe was an obvious target for the termination movement. One of three tribes in the nation with sufficient revenue to meet the annual cost of community services, the Menominees were also able to provide a small yearly payment to each member. The Menominee Tribe was assuredly comfortable, but it was not wealthy—its reserve was just adequate for the scope of a timber operation. Because the tribe was self-sufficient, it was considered for termination." [1]

The dangers of attaining a degree of self-sufficiency are clear, even though termination has been disavowed as the official policy of the Government. James Gamble, a powerful staff member of the Senate Interior and Insular Affairs Committee, occasionally alludes to a list of tribes he has drawn up, deemed ready for termination. Indian opposition to the Indian Resources Act of 1967 (the Omnibus Bill) stemmed from a clear understanding of the implications of attaining competency as advocated by Interior Secretary Udall. Udall said the bill," . . . which would develop initiative, would encourage decision-making, would develop the capacity of Indian groups and leaders to make decisions and would move us down the road toward the right kind of ultimate independence is what the Indian people want." [2]

Asked if "ultimate independence" meant doing away with the reservations, Udall answered: "I think this is undoubtedly the ultimate end result; yes." His testimony came seven years after termination had ceased to be official Government policy.

Indians have failed to push for distribution of claims awards in compensation for property which the Federal Government has taken, lest their payment be viewed as a step toward self-sufficiency. "People are afraid that if they ask for their dollars, the reservation will be terminated," says Roy McIntyre, tribal chairman of the Umatilla Tribe. Sam Deloria, formerly director of the planning office for the Oglala Sioux Tribe in South Dakota, put it more bluntly:

"Indian tribes operate in a reverse carrot-on-a-stick situation. The implied and explicit threat is: 'The minute you guys stop looking like clowns we'll terminate the whole tribe' . . . hence no tribe can enter into a meaningful relationship with the Federal Government . . . without running the risk of annihilation. . . ."

The need for playing dumb extends to the personal level as well. In Oklahoma, for example, an Indian must obtain a certificate of competence to gain control over disposition of his property. If he holds such a certificate, he loses the right to participate in BIA programs and services.

The "incompetent" Indian quickly learns to finesse the system. An Indian woman was denied permission from the BIA to withdraw funds from her private bank account to develop her property and to lease her land. She secured the money, however, by telling the Bureau supervisors she needed it "to feast her kinfolk." No one questioned that explanation. Similarly, Indians who leave the reservation to seek employment find that their attempts at achieving self-sufficiency result in loss of eligibility for free health services and other Indian benefit programs. Upon return to the reservation they may find themselves faced with numerous obstacles to becoming eligible again. The lesson is clear. It pays to remain dependent.

It is better to beg for what is one's by right and to come

as a supplicant for privileges and special favors, than to demand what is due. The Bureau makes it clear that life could be much more unpleasant should the Indians eschew the charity of the BIA and insist upon asserting their rights. In 1964 at a BIA tribal management training program, participating Indians were told flatly not to waste their time going after treaty rights, because the Bureau was doing far more for them than any treaty promised. The message was clear, and the Indians understood.

The tragedy of helplessness.   PAUL CONKLIN

Interior Secretary Udall declined, in 1968, to start litigation to establish the rights of the Paiute Indians to water which they needed to save Pyramid Lake. He rejected their litigation request, saying he could handle it through discretionary powers. Udall added that by persisting, the Indians might impair the ability of the Secretary to help them by administrative authority.[3]

The Bureau controls the "incompetent" Indian's personal trust funds and must countersign his bank withdrawals. The Bureau also knows best how individuals should utilize their property. In one recent instance, an Indian woman said to be aged, ill, and "incompetent," was persuaded by a Bureau official to let him draw money from her private account for plumbing. The official certified a purchase order, had the woman sign for the delivery of plumbing materials to her property, and withdrew the money. The materials were not delivered and the work was never done, although more than three years have passed. The Bureau now tells the woman it is too late to complain.[4]

The Bureau has peculiar notions regarding how best to help Indians: in the State of Washington, the Bureau constructed an all-electric model housing project—but neglected to provide electrical service to the project. The *Tacoma News* reports the following instance:

> "One of the BIA's first jobs was to wire an Indian house for electricity. The family—24 persons live in the five-room house—finally got stark, naked light bulbs and an electric socket in the ancient house. Still, they are using Coleman lanterns and kerosene lamps for light as they must pay $350 to Puget Sound Power and Light Co. before the utility company will run a power line to the house.
> "For 20 years, the family has lived only 500 feet from a power line." [5]

Not even the size of a loan, nor the purpose for which it is used, are decisions for the Indian to make. Often it is easy to borrow $50,000 from the BIA to buy a fishing boat, but difficult to obtain only $3,000 for a fishing net. On the Navajo reservation in Arizona, Indians are required to put up nearly 100 per cent collateral to borrow from the Bureau's revolving fund. Navajos were encouraged to discard a plan for a small cattle-raising business, and instead were urged by the BIA to engage in a clearly unfeasible larger business involving 100 head of cattle.

Not only do Indian enterprises initiated by the Bureau usually lack Indian control; in most instances they are exploitative, paying Indian workers sweatshop wages. A former VISTA volunteer at Wisconsin's Red Cliff Reservation told of a BIA-established shop where tribal women sewed hospital gowns. "In order not to have responsibility for the project, they set it up as a cooperative, with the workers earning only what the profits provided. For a long time only three or four women worked and earned from 25 to 48 cents an hour." When the tribe attempted to unload the losing proposition, the BIA persuaded another tribe to take it over, the VISTA worker said.[6]

Indians have learned however, not to question even gross inequities. For example, as the Indian's banker, the Bureau pays extraordinarily low interest on deposits, sometimes no interest at all. The Bureau as banker fails to credit deposits on time, fails to credit some deposits at all, invests funds in a manner which yields inexcusably low returns, and "borrows" from the Indians' savings at interest rates far below the open market. Indians are deprived of millions of dollars in lost interest alone. The Tyonek Indians of Alaska lost two years' interest on $200,000 because the Bureau withdrew this amount from the Treasury, where it drew a modest four per cent. The money was redeposited in the BIA's regional dispensing account, which draws no interest. The Manchester band of Pomo Indians in California filed suit to contest the BIA's handling of their trust funds, asking payment of interest lost through mismanagement.

The rewards of dependency require more than surrender of control over one's property. The Indian finds that to survive he must surrender his sources of independent leadership. Education, for example, comes at a high price.

"Some students eventually realize the futility of the

struggle by observing what usually happens to the
educated Indian here. In the area of the old Cherokee
Nation, there is really little place for the educated
fullblood. The potential leaders of our tribe really have
but about two choices: that of leaving their own home
and community and try for employment in a community
or state where the Indian is not discriminated against, or
join the white-oriented group by getting a job with the
Indian Bureau, or getting a seat on the chief's executive
committee. This is about the best he can hope to do in
this area." [7]

The individual Indian loses, but the Indian community
loses even more; it is "deprived of its most . . . creative
members [for the] period of bondage as a planned permanent
condition," according to a vice president of the National
Indian Youth Council, Bill Pensoneau. He added, "The
success is measured in terms of how permanently Indians
become removed from their families."

Andrew Dreadfulwater, a Cherokee, sees the BIA as
skimming off the top of potential Indian leadership by
incorporating "good" Indians into the system. "The educated
Cherokee who knows he is a Cherokee tries to help his
people, and immediately he is stopped and loses his job."
The educated Indian who can put his people and his roots
behind him, however, has no such difficulties. These co-
opted leaders reap a variety of rewards—BIA housing, BIA
carpenters to repair their property, BIA scholarships for
their children and even BIA manipulated positions of tribal
leadership—for conforming to what the BIA views as acceptable and progressive standards.

*To survive in the BIA world, the Indian must surrender
all elements of authentic self-government and self determination.* The process starts early, in Indian schools where student government is a sham. It extends to BIA advisory school
boards, which give only the illusion of participating in decisions. Beyond the schools, the tribal councils exhibit many
of the same features of futility and powerlessness. A political
scientist wrote: "A major 'institution' introduced in recent
years into the community [by the BIA] is the tribal govern-

ment. From the viewpoint of the country Sioux, this new institution is 'The Tribe.' In many ways they look at it in the same way that many urban working class look at the police force and city government. They see it as a foreign coercive feature in their daily lives. . . .

"The criterion for selection of tribal councilmen by those few Sioux who do vote in an election is not that the tribal councilman can represent them or their opinion, but because they feel that a particular person knows how to handle whites and can 'get something' for the Sioux. A tribal councilman thus may be tremendously competent or incompetent, socially responsible or irresponsible." [8]

In either event, the council itself is frequently powerless. On the Pine Ridge Reservation in South Dakota: "Local whites are very well aware of who holds the power and the purse strings. . . .And when local whites come to Pine Ridge on business they first go to see the local [BIA] superintendent. A white banker or a mayor of a small town literally has no way to relate to the tribal council and usually no real reason to enter into a relationship." [9]

The BIA office is correctly perceived as the center of authority on the reservation. Sometimes it is much more. On the Salt River Reservation in Utah, the BIA agency building serves as a focal point for the community. BIA administrative and tribal offices, a school, the Presbyterian Church, a gas station, cafe, infirmary, jail, courthouse and other buildings cluster around it.

To thrive, or even to survive, the Indian surrenders his power to criticize. One does not bite the hand that feeds.

In 1966 the Crow Tribal Council in Montana sent the President and the Interior Secretary a list of grievances against their BIA superintendent, asking his removal. Here's what happened:

"Washington officialdom obviously felt that this 'uprising' could not be abetted by the removal of the Superintendent. He stayed. Four months later the Bureau came under renewed Congressional attack for denying the Indians self-government and thereby perpetuating [its] own existence. Termination of the federal responsibilities to the Indians, first proposed by the Eisenhower Administration, again loomed on the horizon. The Crow Tribe called the council together, the first meeting since [the] 'ousting' [of] the superintendent. At this assembly the Tribe voted to send a delegation to Washington to register its anxiety over the threat of 'termination.' They even voted to pay travel expenses for five Tribal delegates *and the Superintendent,* who was unanimously applauded as a persuasive ally." [10] (emphasis added)

Indians are not alone in having cause to fear reprisals for criticizing the BIA. Tribal attorneys, who serve only with the approval of the Secretary of the Interior, also are vulnerable. Critics have been branded troublemakers, communists and "enemies of the Indian." Robert Leland, an attorney in Carson City, Nevada says he uncovered evidence that a land developer, acting in collusion with a BIA official, was attempting to steal land along Pyramid Lake from its Indian owners. When the issue was raised, Leland was suspended without pay from the case while the BIA "investigated" for 14 months. The charges against the land developer were sustained, says Leland, but not until after a series of further bureaucratic maneuvers was he able to resume work for the tribe. University consultants and researchers who have incurred the wrath of the BIA working with community groups have also been ostracized and subjected to libel and slander.

The Indian is required to surrender any potential he might have for economic self-sufficiency. The Bureau has played a key role in permitting, tolerating, even initiating actions which have further limited the resources upon which Indian economic independence might be built. The Bureau consistently sides with the National Park Service and the National Forest Service in efforts to create monuments and public facilities on reservation land. This has happened repeatedly—the creation of a national lakeshore park on the Red Cliff Reservation in Minnesota, a national monument on the Grand Portage Reservation (also in Minnesota), and other lands set aside for national forest reserves in New Mexico, Washington, and Oregon.

Dependency. Incompetency. These are the keys to "help" from the Bureau of Indian Affairs. The rewards of enforced dependency are subtle and seductive:

— The illusion of something for nothing—a cradle-to-the-grave system of services and assistance, based on moral approval for the "good Indian."

— Special avenues for currying favor and receiving privileges. An illusion of individual power and success comes to the Indian who masters the art of manipulation, and thereby wins special approval.

— Relief from the burden of responsibility for one's actions. The BIA is always on hand to save the Indian from himself.

— A shield from anxiety that might come from failure or frustration. The Indian need never consider what he might contribute to society. He never has to confront himself and thus he avoids inner conflict.

— The secret satisfaction of disdaining one's benefactor. By outsmarting his keepers, the Indian preserves his private world of undisplayed emotion.

And these rewards insure an ultimate impasse for the Indian:

". . . By being completely passive, by leaving in the hands of the white society complete responsibility for their problems, [the Indian] would remind the white of his incapacity to solve the problem he had so arrogantly set out to master." [11]

Lesson III: Alienation is Rewarded

The Indian is rewarded with economic security, prestige, power, approval, and material wealth if he is prepared to alienate himself from his land, people, and heritage.

The Bureau handbooks don't say it quite that way. The official and intellectually acceptable formula for alienation states: The Indian must learn the white man's ways so that he can have the best of both worlds.

Performance, learning and achievement are rewarded—by the Bureau. It neglects to say that performance, learning, and achievement, as the Bureau interprets them, mean one thing: rejection of the Indian world.

The Indian is rewarded for rejecting his language. Indian education, in both BIA and public schools, teach that to speak one's native tongue demonstrates ignorance and warrants ridicule. Real Americans must speak English.

> "I often encounter [dorm attendants] who pretend not to speak Navajo. They have become so convinced that speaking Navajo is a bad thing to do that they often won't admit that they can. [Most attendants are themselves products of boarding schools.] The children learn that what they say in Navajo is effectively kept secret from the authorities even if one of the Navajo-speaking members of the staff hears them, because the Navajo staff member will be too ashamed of having understood to tell anyone." [1]

Officials, including some Indian tribal officials, disapprove of efforts to preserve Indian languages by publishing textbooks and newspapers.

The Indian is rewarded for rejecting his birthplace. A prime example is the BIA's relocation program, which recruits Indians to leave the reservation by promising them wonderful jobs and training—far away. The Indian receives a one-way ticket and a relocation allowance. Should he fail or become homesick and leave the program, the Indian finds that the Bureau has set up road blocks and obstacles to keep him from returning home. Those who do return to the reservation are scorned. In BIA lingo, they have gone "back to the blanket" and are regarded with righteous indignation. Returning home, in the BIA's view, is almost unforgivable.

The Bureau assigns its Indian employees to work on reservations, but not on their own reservations. This is justified on grounds of fear of nepotism and an expressed determination to keep BIA employees out of tribal politics. In fact, it operates to insure that the most able Indians are taken away from their reservation—where they might manifest a dangerous empathy for their tribal brother and might even play significant leadership roles while working for the principal, often the sole, source of employment on a reservation.

The Indian is encouraged to reject his parents, and to discount their approval or disapproval. He is taught to turn his back on their values. Father John Bryde, superintendent of Holy Rosary Mission School at Pine Ridge, South Dakota, has observed:

"These kids are learning their values at home unconsciously and operating them at the unconscious level. Then they come to the non-Indian school where the non-Indian values are also taught unconsciously, and there is a conflict.

". . . Indian motivation is not for personal aggrandizement or for personal, self glory, but Indian motivation is that whatever you do you do for the group. So the Indian youngster at home is taught to be unobtrusive. He works with the group. He adjusts to the group. And then he is brought to

A white-owned bar two blocks from Chicago's St. Augustine Indian Center.   ED ECKSTEIN

the school and he is forced to compete on an individual basis.

". . . Another quick answer is this: In the Indian system—kids learn this unconsciously at home—Indians do not judge things by their exteriors, by how they look. In the Indian world view, the whole world is one. It is all related and it is holy, and God is in it. They do not just go by appearances, they go by looking into things. So they judge people and things by what they are instead, and not by what they have, which is a non-Indian system, where you judge a man by the size of his house, by his car, everything like that. So the Indian youngster at home does not get cues like this. . . .

". . .The cues he gets to admire are the people who are old, the people who are good, the people who are kind, the people who are generous, and the people who are wise. It is cues to appreciate these qualities the child gets at home. So he learns to judge people by what they are, not by what they have.

"Then he is sent to school and he is caught in the cultural conflict right there. The dominant value in American culture is material achievement, and the schools are geared to that, reflecting the values of our society. So again, the youngster is plopped into this thing, whose values diametrically oppose the Indian system—material wealth, personal aggrandizement, things like that.

"This is what he is taught at the unconscious level in school, and he gets more conscious of this as he gets older. He looks around him, he sees all the norms by which the dominant society measures success, he sees that he does not have them; he is not wanted; so why go to school, because this school is the means to an end that is impossible or undesirable to him. These are the things in a nutshell." [2]

The Indian is rewarded for rejecting his people and their approval or disapproval. A University of Texas professor of psychiatry says the BIA has created a leadership dilemma for Indians by siphoning off potential leaders, both men and women. "Joining the BIA is and has been a major avenue of social mobility for Indians; however, working for the Bureau limits leadership action and identifies these people as joining the enemy. They lose, as far as leadership is concerned, their influence among their own people."[3]

The Indian is rewarded for rejecting the approval or disapproval of his elders and his peers. A Ponca Indian tells of social isolation which education can bring an Indian: "Indian schools deprive the student of the teaching, experience and counsel of his elders. He is encouraged to realize himself apart from his primary set of communicants and to construe his commitments apart from his loyalties."

> "You must begin anew and put away the wisdom of your fathers. You must lay up food and forget the hungry. When your house is built, your storeroom filled, then look around for a neighbor whom you can take advantage of and seize all he has."—Red Cloud, Chief of the Sioux.

> "There's no way of forcing the younger generation to listen. . . . There's nothing in their studies that includes the traditions and the customs of our people."—Henry Old Coyote, a member of the Crow Tribe.[5]

> "I was visiting an Indian school and a movie was being shown in the auditorium about the cavalry and the Indians. The cavalry was, of course, outnumbered and holding an impossible position where the Indians had chased them into the rocks. The Indians, attempting to sneak up on the cavalry, were being killed, one every shot. When it finally appeared that the Indians were going to overrun the army position the ubiquitous cavalry appeared on the far horizon with their bugle blowing, and charged in to save the beleaguered few. The whole auditorium full of Indian students cheered."[6]

The Indian is rewarded if he rejects his people's standards of achievements, performance and contribution. This is illustrated in the conflict between urban and Indian values in an industrial context. Nationally, there has been a major effort to promote members of minority groups to supervisory positions in industry, but the Indian has fared poorly. In several instances, Indians have quit jobs when promoted or given new responsibilities. It appears there is a clash of

BOB ADELMAN

values. Indians generally are not aggressive, and thus tend to be non-competitive in an employment or a school situation. An Indian is reluctant to accept a promotion which might make him superior in status to those whom he regards as his peers.

The Indian who performs and achieves is rewarded. But for every reward, there is a price. The educated Indian alienates himself from his people, and at a point ceases to be even a sufficient showpiece for whites. Tillie Walker, a Mandan Indian and director of the United Scholarship Service of Denver, Colorado, recalls a student who told her, "A few years ago everyone was asking 'where are the young articulate Indians who will speak out?' Now that we're ready to speak, they say, 'Where are the Indian people from the grassroots?' "

But another Indian youth found no contradiction in the rejection of the educated Indian. "In Ponca City [Oklahoma], there is a group of white people who make money dressing up in Indian costumes and doing Indian dances. These people avoid Indians in the same town like the plague. Our artifacts are more real to them than we are." [7]

The price paid for rewards in the white man's world takes many forms: loss of identity, loss of family, even loss of life. Dr. Robert Roessel, Jr., Vice President of the Navajo Community College at Many Farms, Arizona, tells of a young Cheyenne who worked with him at the Indian Education Center at Arizona State University. He had just been discharged from the Marines and his wife was attending the university. One night the young man, George Harris, committed suicide.

"Roberta Harris [said] that her husband had nothing to live for. He was a person with a high school education, a person who was an outstanding basketball player; he was a person well liked by nearly everyone, and yet he had nothing to live for. Roberta explained that her husband didn't know who he was and in the process of acquiring this excellent education, lost himself—in fact was ashamed of his Indian heritage."

For others, the price is higher than life. Death would be an easy price to pay. There is no going back.

"I come not with malice but with a conscience and desperation. I cannot sit quietly and witness the terrible tolls in wasted human life, lives of young Indians—my own family—that comes from the failures of the Indian-help programs that engulf our every activity. Always these failures are the Indian's fault. Always we must change ourselves to suit the fancies of our providers.

"We are totally administered. We can experience nothing directly but death. So we have turned to death . . . by drinking on railroad tracks in Ponca City and greeting our salvation train. We drown ourselves in wine and smother our brains in glue. The only time we are free is when we're drunk. I am speaking of my flesh and blood and of this hour. Yet there is another walking death that we are driven to—social death." [8]

Part Three

THE BARRIERS
TO CHANGE

The governmental practices and policies which work against the American Indian are long-established, deeply entrenched. In the Agriculture Department, the Public Health Service, Interior and elsewhere—but especially in the Bureau of Indian Affairs—they operate to alienate the Indian to perpetuate his dependency and to thwart his every attempt at self-realization. Often these practices run directly counter to official policy; they stymie presidential or congressional directives. Yet they endure, seemingly with a life of their own.

Good men go into the BIA, but years later their bright hopes for reform have dimmed, their sense of outrage and moral indignation has become deadened.

Why is this? What happens? Must this continue? These are the questions which must be explored. The Bureau says its hands are tied, that it lacks the legal authority to make the needed changes in policy and practice. The Bureau, however, has all the legislative authority it needs, perhaps considerably more than it should have. These administrative practices, policies and regulations which have assumed the authority of truth could be altered by the stroke of a pen.

No agency in the Federal Government has more leeway to do good or evil than the Bureau of Indian Affairs. Its history is a story of paths not chosen. Witness this mandate:

> "The Commissioner of Indian Affairs shall, under the direction of the Secretary of the Interior, and agreeably to such regulations as the President may prescribe, have the management of all Indian affairs and of all matters arising out of Indian relations." (—from United States legal statutes.) [1]

The BIA could contract out virtually all of its functions to Indians today, and thereby eliminate many of the chores the Government now performs. Federal law clearly states:

> "Where any of the tribes are, in the opinion of the Secretary of the Interior, competent to direct the employment of their . . . mechanics teachers, farmers, or such persons engaged for them, the direction of such persons may be given to the proper authority of the tribe." [2]

> "The Secretary of the Interior is authorized, in his discretion, to enter into a contract or contracts with any State *or Territory,* or political *subdivision thereof,* or with any State university, college, or school, or *with any appropriate State or private corporation,* agency, or institution, for the education, medical attention, agricultural assistance, and social welfare, including relief of distress of Indians in such State or Territory. . . ." (emphasis added) [3]

A tribal government can constitute a territory or political subdivision for purposes of this act and a group of Indians—or a tribe—could establish a private corporation under State law for purposes of entering into contracts.

Whether it would be wise for the Bureau to do so is another question, because the Bureau has failed to equip the Indian with adequate education, training, technical expertise or managerial experience. The contracting out device also could become simply a way of abdicating federal responsibilities. The only point being made here is that the Bureau has the power.

The Bureau has the power to make Bureau officials— including Area Directors and Superintendents—accountable to the Indians they serve. In one or two isolated instances the Bureau has permitted the tribe to interview candidates for Superintendent, but could do far more. It could require genuine participation by Indians in the decision-making processes which so deeply affect their lives.

The Bureau has the power to enable tribes to consolidate their landholdings, to develop assets and to assist in the development of land which has been fallow because of heirship litigation or checkerboarding. The BIA can invest trust funds for a substantial return and make trust funds available for investment in Indian projects, subject to appropriate safeguards. The Secretary of the Interior has "discovered" that he has the power to consolidate tribal land through the Bureau of Land Management.[4] That power could be delegated to the Commissioner of Indian Affairs. None of these reforms is being done, although some are quite simple. Consolidation of land may involve complex procedures, but urban renewal agencies deal with similar problems daily. The BIA has the power and could have the funds, if it moved flexibly in its treatment of Indian land and trust accounts as collateral for loans to purchase heirship land.

Under the Indian Reorganization Act of 1934 the BIA has not only the power, but also the obligation, to permit tribes to participate in the drawing up of their own budgets, establishing their own priorities. The tribe has the legal right to take the initiative, draw up its own budget and balance the available resources to best meet its needs—not just at the preliminary stage but at the point of final submission.

The BIA has the duty to see that every Indian is provided with a lawyer in both civil and criminal cases.

> "In all States and Territories where there are reservations or allotted Indians the United States attorney shall represent them in all suits at law and in equity." [5]

The Bureau has the power to reorganize and restructure itself to be responsive to the needs of today. These powers could extend, but are not so limited, to delegating greater authority at the reservation level, eliminating red tape, revising the laws which apply to Indians and renouncing termination as a Government policy. Without any new laws the BIA can do such things as initiate procedures to assure that Indian funds earmarked for public facilities (such as roads) are spent in ways that actually benefit the Indians; enforce preferential employment guarantees for Indians in Government contracts; train Indians to better manage their assets and affairs free of Government paternalism; protect the Indian from unfair state and local taxation and assure him his rightful share of state and local services. Equally important, the Bureau could allow the tribes greater latitude in designing their tribal governments and delegate more authority to those governments. Certainly the Bureau could cease practices which discriminate against Indians in favor of Bureau employees.

As Helen Mitchell, former recording secretary of the National Congress of American Indians, told BIA Commissioner Robert Bennett at a Regional meeting at Spokane, Washington:

> "I firmly believe that legislation is not necessary but in a very few items. The NCAI Executive Committee, and other leaders, sat around a table and took a cross section of Indian country. We found that what can't be done in the Portland Area is being done in [the] Aberdeen Area, and what can't be done in [the] Aberdeen Area is being done in Phoenix and so on down the line. I suggest, Mr. Commissioner, that the power is within your reach." [6]

The authority is there; at times, BIA officials have admitted it. Commissioner Bennett, in Albuquerque shortly before his term ended, said: "I believe as we look over the authority we already have, that Congress has already given us, we can make greater delegation of this authority . . . to the Superintendents so there can be quicker decision-making to enable Indian people to take advantage of the opportunities they now have." [7]

Bennett also declared that he expects no difficulties in securing cooperation from Congress. He said, "I hope we can work with the Congress to get these opportunities for you to make more decisions. . . . The atmosphere and the environment for Indian opportunity is much better than it has ever been. There is much good will in the Congress. . . ."

Given this power to act, what then are the real sources of resistance to change? We shall analyze three areas:

— *The structure of the Bureau itself.*

— *The Bureau's lowly position within the Interior Department.*

— *The politics of Indians vs. the politics of resource development.*

PRESENT STRUCTURE OF THE BUREAU OF INDIAN AFFAIRS

ASSISTANTS TO COMMISSIONER

COMMISSIONER
DEPUTY COMMISSIONER

CONG' RELATIONS, INFORMATION & INSPECTION OFFICERS

ASST. COMMR. COMMUNITY SERVICES — 2 STAFFS 5 DIVS.

ASST. COMMR. ECONOMIC DEVELOPMENT — 3 DIVS.

ASST. COMMR. EDUCATION — 3 STAFFS 5 DIVS.

ASST. COMMR. ADMINISTRATION — DATA CENTER 3 STAFFS 6 DIVS.

ASST. COMMR. ENGINEERING — 3 DIVS.

ASST. COMMR. PROGRAM COORDINATION — 2 DIVS.

AREA DIRECTOR

ASST. DIR. COMMUNITY SERVICES — AREA BRANCH OFFICERS

ASST. DIR. ECONOMIC DEVELOPMENT — AREA BRANCH OFFICERS

ASST. DIR. EDUCATION — AREA BRANCH OFFICERS

ASST. DIR. ADMINISTRATION — AREA BRANCH OFFICERS

ASST. DIR. ENGINEERING — AREA BRANCH OFFICERS

ASST. DIR. PROGRAM COORDINATION — AREA BRANCH OFFICERS

AGENCY SUPERINTENDENT

BRANCH OFFICERS AND STAFFS

BRANCH OFFICERS AND STAFFS

I

THE BIA—A TERMINAL CASE OF BUREAUCRACY

Judged by four basic standards of governmental performance—efficiency, technical competence, innovation or effective advocacy—the Bureau of Indian Affairs is a failure. It appears remiss in meeting even the minimal standards of performance for a public body entrusted with a public function.

This is not an attack on the motives, intentions or character of BIA employees, however. The Bureau has a number of sincere, dedicated civil servants. It also has accumulated over the years unique stores of experience and expertise in dealing with Indian people and their problems.

In a 1969 report to the White House, Alvin M. Josephy, Jr. quoted Leon Osview's memo to the Subcommittee on Indian Education: "The BIA structure is designed more than most for stability. It is doubtful that very much could be done with or to the people in the organization, given the present structure, to encourage innovative practice. . . . One thing does seem certain: the present structure not only serves to reward unaggressive behavior and docility but punishes, usually by transfer, those who persist in behaving like leaders. The reward system of BIA discourages leadership, on purpose. It is, therefore, not possible to conceive of change and improvement within the present structure." [1]

Besides the Bureau's wealth of official powers, it has been given a sweeping mandate to reform itself. When BIA Commissioner Robert Bennett took office in May 1966, President Johnson told him: "Do anything you have to do" to straighten up the BIA. "If there are cobwebs in the Bureau, then clean them out. Let's set up some Civil Service Boards to hear the cases. Let's get some can-do people at work." Bennett went out of office in June 1969. Bureaucratic inertia had triumphed; the BIA was more lethargic than ever. Former Interior Secretary Udall criticized this lethargy, noting that the BIA seems ". . . to have a time clock of its own . . . it is hard to get the feeling that anything is urgent."

A Kennedy Administration Task Force was alarmed by the degree of dissatisfaction among Indians over the BIA's network of reviews, appeals and form-swapping. Five years later, at a 1966 Indian Leaders Conference with Commissioner Bennett at Spokane, Washington, spokesmen for the Umatilla Tribe said their efforts at self-help were "continually frustrated by administrative delays, indecisiveness, foot-dragging and over-concern with technicalities in the Bureau of Indian Affairs. . . ." The red tape permeates every layer of the Bureau's activity, especially its decentralized area offices.

When former Commissioner Bennett tried to circumvent his own bureaucracy by contracting with outside parties for the provision of services, he was thwarted by "delays," "indecisiveness" and a reluctance by field officials to approve contracts without seeking endless prior clearances from above.

Again Josephy quoted from Osview: "In theory, a major advantage of decentralization is that it permits a freer exercise of political democracy. . . . It would be satisfying to be able to note that such an advantage inheres in the BIA administrative structure. But the route upward through the echelons seems to be no less difficult than downward for personnel, at least on the things that matter most." Josephy said the BIA's organization runs roughshod over grassroots efforts and specialists' advice, to the advantage of the administrative structure.[2] The result is a system of endless buckpassing, with many minor local questions winding up in Washington.

Reluctance to delegate authority to the local level also is crippling. The local superintendent, for example, can approve sales up to so many board-feet of Indian timber, but beyond he must have the consent of his area director. The area director also has a limit, beyond which he must turn to the BIA Commissioner. Even the Commissioner is restricted; final authority for large timber sales rests with the Secretary of the Interior. In one year some 83 per cent of all sales by volume required the Secretary's approval—a process which delays the sales and inhibits negotiations in the up-and-down lumber market.

With notable exceptions, the quality of BIA personnel remains low, its level of incompetency alarmingly high. Interviews with officials in other Government agencies, consultants and specialists and academics bear out this charge of pervasive mediocrity made long ago by the Indians.

Studies by the General Accounting Office, internal BIA Reports and a myriad of task force findings all point to an incredibly low level of technical competence at the Bureau. Despite the criticism, the Bureau has been reluctant to reorganize itself, and slow to hire outside consultants and expert help. The Department of the Interior, and especially the BIA, spend considerably smaller percentages of their budgets on consultants and specialists than most other agencies.

As a result of this closed-door policy toward consultants and a reluctance to restructure, the research and statistical capability of the Bureau is poor. A recent independent study of BIA manpower programs said the agency "has no really hard data on population dynamics, income, employment, education, and so forth. It has few benchmarks against which to measure progress, and more importantly, grossly inadequate data on which to base economic development and manpower programs." [3] Equally shocking, the report said, is the "total absence of any research and demonstration funds in the BIA budget. A sensitivity to social science research and the linkages between Research and Demonstration and program innovation has not existed in the past in the BIA."

Other studies have made the same observation. Record keeping and statistics remain low priority at the BIA. Instances have been reported where records were deliberately destroyed, during GAO investigations and other research projects, to hide evidence of poor BIA performance.

The BIA substitutes excuses for performance. Recruiting is difficult, the Bureau says, because the work is mostly in remote areas; because pay is low and non-competitive; because there is little prestige and a high frustration potential.

Admittedly there is little prestige in working for the Bureau. No job market is clamoring for ex-BIA employees. The Peace Corps and VISTA have encountered little difficulty, however, in recruiting talented men and women of all ages and backgrounds to work for subsistence pay and travel to the most isolated and remote spots in the United States and elsewhere. The problem at the BIA goes to the nature of the BIA worker's role, which relates to the high frustration potential.

The Bureau's admission of recruiting difficulties is in itself a characterization of much that is wrong. The prime untapped sources are the Indians desiring to live on the reservations and contribute to the well-being of their people. But the Bureau has not trained them to assume high-level managerial positions. In 1968, 89 per cent of the Indians employed by the BIA held positions that paid less than $8,000.

The Bureau has been reluctant to contract with tribal councils to perform certain functions. When it has, tribal employees have been paid lower salaries and treated as inferior to Bureau employees. Finally, employment in the Bureau, for an Indian, is often viewed as a sellout—a choice between siding with his people or joining the enemy. And under the circumstances, the recruitment problem is really a reflection of the Bureau's relationship to the Indian.

A "New Day" for Indians is unveiled every two-to-four years—during each Presidential campaign, upon the appointment of a new BIA Commissioner, and upon creation of each new study task force.

The "New Day" invariably is old policy swaddled in new rhetoric, pumping more dollars through the same cumbersome and incompetent bureaucracy. There is always talk about "self-determination." Josephy in his report to President Nixon quotes an anonymous Indian leader as saying, "During the last eight years, Indian policies and programs have been studied to death. What we need is for someone to begin paying attention to some of the things that the Indians recommended in those studies."

One major source of resistance to innovation is the process which imposes review upon review on every idea proposed from the top. The process subjects each creative spark to attack and distortion by persons who see their empires threatened. Even if innovation were encouraged, however, a jungle of regulations, procedures and guidelines which have not been streamlined in 30 years poses a formidable obstacle.

> "How do we develop new techniques, the opportunity to enable tribes . . . to make their estates more valuable? Here again we have been shackled with the rigidity of our rules and present policy. Let me give an example. . . .
>
> "When one of the big dams on the Columbia River (in Washington State) was built and the [Umatilla] tribe received a large settlement, the ones who remained on the reservation and who wanted to further develop their reservation resources came up to me with what was a very creative idea; this was six-seven years ago. They wanted to take the money and, instead of dividing it up per capita, to buy out the interests in the Indian reservation of those Indians who no longer lived on the reservation and who would prefer in that period to take cash. This, of course, would make the reservation more viable. The Bureau of Indian Affairs said there was no way to *do* it. Indeed, there was not at the time. But how can you solve economic and human problems unless you can solve problems like this? (Statement by Interior Secretary Udall, April 14, 1966, at Santa Fe, New Mexico)

Ironically, Udall's example proves he *did* have the power to respond. He was restricted, if at all, only by a regulation he himself could have waived. But he was trapped because he took the word of his own bureaucracy that there was nothing he could do.

Massive resistance to innovation comes from within the BIA. It is there paternalism and empire-building remain the rule, despite decades of lip-service to self-determination for the Indians. It will be difficult to change these deep-seated attitudes, the Pyramid Lake Tribal Council wrote Udall in 1967. "Many of the 22,000 government employees directly employed in Indian matters . . . are set in their ways. It may prove impossible to convert government overseers with 'father knows best' attitudes into public servants willing and competent to work for those members of the public who are Indians." [4]

Commissioner Bennett spent a major portion of his nearly three years in office trying to soften attitudes within the Bureau. He created a BIA newsletter, "The Indian Record," for distribution to Indians and lower echelons of the Bureau in the hope of strengthening understanding.

Such evangelical endeavors are certain to fail, however, as long as BIA powers are fragmented in the present decentralized system. Upward accountability stops at each step of the way. It is like a cliff pocked with tiny platforms, each isolated from those above and below. From these platforms, BIA personnel can fight among themselves and shout at those above and below, secure in the knowledge that they are out of reach. The Indian, at the foot of the cliff, is limited in his shouting range. He is rarely heard beyond the lowest platform.

The Bureau has even thwarted the traditional method of balancing "staff against line" where professionals directly accountable to the leadership serve a watchdog role over line personnel to insure accountability upward. The passage of time has merely produced parallel bureaucracies, neither of which is accountable, both of which spend most of their time fighting each other.

In budgeting BIA monies, the structure becomes even more uncoordinated. A 1969 study noted:

"In the budget process, each agency, in theory, prepares its own budget, which is then evaluated by the area office and consolidated into an area budget, then submitted to the Washintgon office for similar evaluation and consolidation. In practice, guidelines based upon previous budgets are determined in Washington, and allocations are actually dictated and controlled by the Divisions as entities rather than by the agencies at the operational level. For example, if a superintendent decides that the budget of one branch on his reservation should be cut and another increased in order to serve a tribe more effectively, the offended branch sends word up through the line to its Division chief in Washington, who then informs the superintendent that if his branch does not need the money in his agency, it will be transferred within the same branch to another agency. Under this system, considerable time and energy that should be spent on service at the operational level are expended in conflicts between the Division hierarchies on the one hand, and the superintendents and area directors on the other. At the same time, the system often results in the presence on reservations of branch specialists who are not needed and, conversely, of not enough personnel or funding for branches that are badly needed." [5]

Officials who want to develop an idea or speed up a process must learn to lose more often than they win, and especially to expect defeat on innovative suggestions. The result is complete frustration of leadership and creative work at every level.

In the Bureau of Indian Affairs, the Indian has no advocate. The BIA seems incapable of fighting either for adequate resources or for self-determination for the Indians. Each new commissioner takes over administration of the BIA, undaunted and unaware of the Bureau's capacity to undercut him completely. Taking office in 1961, President Kennedy's appointee Philleo Nash, was warned that "many of our leading Commissioners . . . have become the captives of the professionals with the Bureau." "I am not," Nash replied confidently, "proposing to be anybody's captive."

Senator Clinton Anderson of New Mexico responded:

> "I will tell you privately some time of an Indian Commissioner who assured me that he would not become a captive and after about a year he said, 'I'm very sorry, there is nothing I can do. They send me to Alaska one week. They send me to Guam the next week. The people here get me out—they will not let me sit here in the office.' "

Organizational changes designed to sharpen the BIA's responsiveness to Indians instead become new instruments of control in the hands of veteran bureaucrats. BIA officials who try to deal responsibly with Indian demands and needs, who make a genuine effort to advocate the Indians' point of view, find themselves without power, boxed in by regulations and fellow workers. In most cases the official who knows most about a tribal situation and may be most responsive to tribal demands, the superintendent, lacks the authority to deal with it.

In the state of Washington, for example, the Quinault Indians complained that while the superintendent of the Western Washington agency was sympathetic to their pleas for protection of their land base and for greater self-determination, the Portland Area Office of the BIA constantly vetoed the superintendent's determination.[6]

The bulk of BIA employees are dependent upon Area Offices for promotions, transfers, information, access to Washington and help with technical projects on their reservations. Thus, Bureau employees who dare to side with the Indians against the wishes of the Area Office must be prepared to face stern reprisal from which there is no effective protection.

A memorandum from an acting reservation superintendent to his area director mentioned the three worlds of the reservation—the BIA, the Indian and the local non-Indian: "Many of the non-Indian employees lack the capacity or desire to understand why the Indians' behavior and points of view differ from their own. They do not wish to communicate with Indians on a social plane. They work with

Indians during the day, but on their own time they associate with the BIA fraternity or, to a far lesser degree, with members of the local white community." [7]

BIA field employees often are transferred when they begin bucking standard operating procedures. A group of tribal leaders meeting in Albuquerque complained to Commissioner Bennett about "the harrassment of some Bureau employees who become *too* involved with the Indians. Many of these people are highly qualified and dedicated to helping the Indian people, but because these individuals buck the old-fashioned Bureau policies, the Bureau rewards them by transferring them out of the Area or into another department. . . . Local Area officials [should not] abuse these individuals. . . ." [8] Bennett heard similar complaints from Indian representatives at a conference in Las Vegas, Nevada.

Ultimately, the only persons with an enduring interest in making the Bureau more responsive are the Indians. Officials come and go. Policy changes, but the sluggishness remains. The Bureau's constant dampening of all efforts at Indian involvement, Indian initiative, Indian participation are the true tell-tale symptoms of a bureaucracy in its terminal stages. Josephy's White House Report said it bluntly:

> "On the reservation level, where Indians are trying to participate constructively to help frame, design and execute programs to meet their problems, they are hamstrung and frustrated daily by an endless round of delays and negativism occasioned by the internal workings of the higher echelons of the Bureau. The effect is that the Indians cannot participate in making decisions for themselves, for in meaningful things, the decisions cannot be made at their level. Government protestations in support of the principle of self-determination notwithstanding, the important decisions must be, and are, made—under the present arrangement—in the echelons above the Indians."

DEPARTMENT OF THE INTERIOR

Organization chart of the Department of the Interior.

THE SECRETARY OF THE INTERIOR / THE UNDER SECRETARY

OFFICE FOR EQUAL OPPORTUNITY
JOB CORPS COORDINATION
OFFICE OF ECOLOGY
OFFICE OF THE SCIENCE ADVISER
OFFICE OF WATER RESOURCES RESEARCH
OFFICE OF INFORMATION
OFFICE OF PROGRAM ANALYSIS
PROGRAM SUPPORT STAFF
OIL IMPORTS APPEALS BOARD
BOARD OF CONTRACT APPEALS

SOLICITOR
— OFFICE OF THE SOLICITOR

ASSISTANT SECRETARY — ADMINISTRATION
- OFFICE OF MANAGEMENT OPERATIONS
- OFFICE OF SURVEY AND REVIEW
- OFFICE OF BUDGET
- OFFICE OF MANAGEMENT RESEARCH
- OFFICE OF PERSONNEL MANAGEMENT
- OFFICE OF LIBRARY SERVICES

ASSISTANT SECRETARY — FISH AND WILDLIFE AND PARKS
COMMISSIONER OF FISH AND WILDLIFE
- BUREAU OF COMMERCIAL FISHERIES
- BUREAU OF SPORT FISHERIES AND WILDLIFE
- NATIONAL PARK SERVICE

ASSISTANT SECRETARY — MINERAL RESOURCES
- OIL IMPORT ADMINISTRATION
- OFFICE OF OIL AND GAS
- OFFICE OF COAL RESEARCH
- OFFICE OF MINERALS AND SOLID FUELS
- GEOLOGICAL SURVEY
- BUREAU OF MINES

ASSISTANT SECRETARY — PUBLIC LAND MANAGEMENT
- BUREAU OF INDIAN AFFAIRS
- BUREAU OF LAND MANAGEMENT
- BUREAU OF OUTDOOR RECREATION
- OFFICE OF TERRITORIES

ASSISTANT SECRETARY — WATER AND POWER DEVELOPMENT
DEFENSE ELECTRIC POWER ADMINISTRATION
- BUREAU OF RECLAMATION
- BONNEVILLE POWER ADMINISTRATION
- SOUTHEASTERN POWER ADMINISTRATION
- SOUTHWESTERN POWER ADMINISTRATION
- ALASKA POWER ADMINISTRATION

ASSISTANT SECRETARY — WATER POLLUTION CONTROL
OFFICE OF SALINE WATER
- FEDERAL WATER POLLUTION CONTROL ADMINISTRATION

II

THE COMPROMISED ADVOCATE: THE BIA WITHIN THE DEPARTMENT OF THE INTERIOR

The U.S. Department of the Interior is a chamber of the mighty. Oil and gas billionaires, lumber barons, ranchers and corporate farmers, sportsmen and recreation interests, hydroelectric and mining promoters number among its customary clientele and constituency. All have intimate relationships with the Department, all work amicably with Interior officials to cultivate a relationship of mutual accommodation. The Indian, however, stands out as the poor relation—ill at ease, an incongruous and unwanted guest evoking condescension and embarrassment. The Bureau of Indian Affairs is perhaps the lowliest of agencies housed within Interior, even though it receives a little more than 18 per cent of the Department's budget and employs almost 25 per cent of the Department's staff.

The BIA's location within the Department of the Interior is fundamentally incompatible with the effective discharge of its duty to Indians.

Interior's jurisdictions include the Bureau of Commercial Fisheries, the Bureau of Sports Fisheries and Wildlife, the National Park Service, Bureau of Mines, U.S. Geological Survey, Bureau of Land Management, Bureau of Outdoor Recreation and Bureau of Reclamation—each of them enjoying the support of well-organized and well-formed local interest, with strong congressional liaison.

—The Bureau of Mines opposed Indian interests when it sought to obtain helium from the Navajo Indians in the Southwest at a low price.

—The Bureau of Commercial Fisheries and the Bureau

of Sport Fisheries and Wildlife are in conflict with the Indians over Indian fishing rights, including the salmon controversy in the Northwest.

—The Bureau of Reclamation has consistently opposed efforts by the Paiute Indians in Nevada to protect Pyramid Lake.

—The Bureau of Land Management is in disagreement with the Colorado River Tribe in Arizona and the Fort Mojave Tribe in California as the tribes seek to protect the boundaries of their reservations.

—The National Parks Service has eyes for the Bad Lands, which belong to the Oglala Sioux Indians on Pine Ridge Reservation, South Dakota.

And beyond Interior, the BIA has constant difficulties with such other land-oriented agencies as the National Forest Service (part of the Agriculture Department) and the U.S. Corps of Engineers.

Inter-agency and even intra-agency disagreements in Washington are not uncommon. Critical to their outcome is the forum in which the differences are judged. Within the Department of the Interior, the Indian generally loses. His interests, as represented by the Bureau, get short shrift in that forum.

Indians invariably are forced to give way to more powerful interests. Both in specific controversies involving a dam or a park, and in departmental controversies involving budget, personnel and priorities, the BIA structurally lacks the research capacity, the technical expertise and the legal counsel needed to present fully the Indian case. Most of the time it must rest on expert opinion from elsewhere—and often the experts come from the agency with whom the Bureau is in conflict. In a dispute involving oil, the BIA will seek advice from the U.S. Geological Survey, knowing full well that the USGS interests lie with the oil industry.

Many issues hinge upon a consideration of the comparative cost, the feasibility and the efficiency of alternative solutions. It is cheaper, for example, to build a dam on Indian land—if one does not consider the cost of relocation, social disorganization and rising welfare dependency. The BIA lacks the technicians needed to build a convincing case against such a decision.

Although the BIA is the Indian's advocate, the BIA's legal advice comes from lawyers out of Interior Department's Solicitor's Office, which serves the entire Department. Indian interests are not approached from the perspective of Indian rights—but rather as matters for administrative resolution involving the balancing of competing interests. Rights are not weighed in that balancing. They are considered only after the best accommodation has been reached—and it is necessary to prepare legal memoranda demonstrating that the decision involves no curtailment of Indian rights.

In Josephy's report to the White House, the Solicitor's Office was singled out as a major source of resistance and opposition to BIA progress. "We lose a lot of battles there," a BIA official admitted.

In Department disputes, the BIA often finds itself advocating the Indian's cause before an administrator who is biased, unknowledgeable and frequently hostile.

Within the Department and under the Secretary, there are six assistant secretaries, whose jurisdiction are water and power, public land management, wildlife and parks, mineral resources, water pollution control, and administration. The Commissioner of Indian Affairs, head of the BIA, does not have the rank of an assistant secretary, or even of a deputy assistant secretary. The BIA falls under the deputy to the Assistant Secretary for Public Land Management— literally low man on the totem pole. Even when the dispute is with the BIA's co-equal, the Bureau of Land Management, the overall land orientation of the Interior Department weighs against the Indians.

In disputes outside that division, the BIA finds itself outranked. Even if the assistant secretary or under-secretary heading the disputing agency is neutral toward the BIA, the Indians are likely to lose because they are politically impotent and because the BIA's inadequacies are so widely known that it often is assumed to be wrong.

The land and economic orientation of the Department also operates to downgrade Indian cultural, social and religious factors. To take them seriously is considered "soft-headed" and romantic, and such views are difficult to defend in a review by the Secretary, the Bureau of the Budget or a congressional committee.

It is inconsistent with the Secretary of the Interior's overall responsibilities for him to be neutral or impartial, let alone sympathetic, to the Indian's cause. He cannot be an impartial arbiter because his primary responsibility as a Cabinet member is as an advocate for conservation and as the administrator charged with protecting natural resources. He must mediate between demands to use and exploit our natural resources and demands to preserve them as part of an irreplaceable heritage. These concerns limit the terms and context in which the Secretary can consider Indian affairs. Matters of culture, of human welfare, of social cost, of self-determination and sovereignty are given less weight in a search for the best use of land and natural resources. The greatest good for the greatest number is the rule, and in terms of land use it is unlikely to produce a decision that favors a few scattered, politically powerless Indians.

Even a Secretary such as Stewart Udall, who held a deep personal commitment to Indians, found that his official overriding duties, commitments and priorities precluded adequate consideration for the Indians. On leaving office in January, 1969, Udall told Interior employees that his only regret was that he had "not done enough for Indians."

Yet, Udall's commitment to and concern for the well-being of Indians was the reason why two Presidential Task Forces did not recommend removal of the Bureau from the Department of Interior. With Udall gone, the National Congress of American Indians, meeting at Albuquerque on May 6, 1969, for the first time felt free to call for removing the Bureau of Indian Affairs and giving it independent agency status noting: "The Secretary of the Interior often finds himself hamstrung by the Department and other interests. . . . This conflict of interest at the Secretarial level cannot contribute to the fair and impartial administration of Indian Affairs." [1]

Even when the Secretary of the Interior is personally sympathetic to the Indian cause, he is not free to act upon his personal philosophy and overrule the decisions of those who are less sympathetic. A degree of delegation, of reliance on the judgment of subordinates, is necessary in running an agency so vast as the Department of the Interior. This delegation of authority carries with it a presumption in favor of sustaining the initial decision of the official. To second-guess and overrule a subordinate often does irreparable injury to morale and administration. The 1969 report to the White House pointed out another administrative problem for the Secretary:

> "[T]he ability of the Secretary to play a decisive role in Indian affairs is weakened when he goes through the Assistant Secretary for Public Land Management to the Commissioner of Indian Affairs. The record of the last two administrations [the Kennedy and Johnson Administrations] was one of continued poor communication and 'slippage' between the Secretary and the Bureau. On many occasions, the Secretary gave orders, only to discover months later that nothing had been done or, in some cases, that the exact opposite of what he had requested had taken place."

Any Secretary of the Interior, as a Presidential appointee, is a political figure. He is keenly aware that the Indian has no political clout, that the Bureau of Indian Affairs is unpopular, and that he must face hostile examiners at the Bureau of the Budget in fighting for money to help the Indians. It is here, at the Budget office, that the duties of the Secretary as the chief conservationist conflict most harshly with his duty to the Indian. Two principal examiners at the Bureau of the Budget, Harry McKittrick and Earl Darrah, are known within Washington circles to be unsympathetic to the Indian's welfare and unresponsive to considerations of Indian community development, social welfare and cultural diversity. Nevertheless, they reign supreme on questions of funds for Indian matters, partly by virtue of long tenure and partly because they define the considerations and justifications which must be demonstrated to win their approval. In addition, over the years, McKittrick and Darrah have developed a close working relationship with James Gamble, a staff member at the Senate Committee on Interior and Insular Affairs, and a rabid terminationist. For some time, Gamble has been able to block constructive program proposals or secure budgetary cuts before the program ever reached Congress, with the aid of McKittrick and Darrah. President Johnson, in a message to Congress on March 6, 1968, announced that he was directing the Secretary of the Interior to establish and train Indian parent school boards for federal Indian schools. The President's message was in response to recommendations from a broad cross-section of Indians, non-Indian educators and a special Interagency Task Force of the Government. In spite of this support, it is said that the Bureau of the Budget balked at certain aspects of the proposal and, as a result, inhibited the BIA from effectively implementing the Presidential directive.[2]

Part of the power of examiners in the Bureau of the Budget lies in their anonymity. The Indian may not know who his enemies are, but the BIA certainly does.

III

WINNING THE WEST: CONGRESS' UNFINISHED BUSINESS

Beyond the Interior Department and the Bureau of the Budget the Indian confronts an even greater obstacle to self-realization and survival: the United States Congress.

Legislative proposals dealing with Indian affairs largely fall within the jurisdiction of Senate and House committees on Interior and Insular Affairs. Like the Department of the Interior, the committees are land oriented. The committees are stacked with Western congressmen, whose districts are witnessing rapid development. That development threatens the Indian.

Every member of the Senate Committee on Interior and Insular Affairs, and all but seven of the members of the House Committee, come from west of the Mississippi. Senate committee members include Senators Jackson of Washington, Anderson of New Mexico, Burdick of North Dakota, Bible of Nevada, Church of Idaho, Moss of Utah, McGovern of South Dakota, Nelson of Wisconsin, Metcalf of Montana, Allott of Colorado, Jordan of Idaho, Fannin of Arizona, Hansen of Wyoming, Hatfield of Oregon, Gravel of Alaska, Stevens of Alaska, and Bellmon of Oklahoma. The House Committee has 34 members and is chaired by Rep. Wayne N. Aspinall of Colorado.

Even the Interior Appropriations Subcommittees in the House and Senate are heavily Western. This geographic bias is a product of the vast role the Federal Government as property owner, developer, manager or conservator plays in the Western United States. The Federal Government owns 86.7 per cent of the land in Nevada, for example, 44.6 per cent in Arizona, 66.8 per cent in Utah, 64.2 per cent in Idaho.

In these states, where sparse populations and water shortages long have retarded growth, a new prosperity is developing. Every major economic interest in the West and Far West finds itself coveting the Indian's few remaining resources in the race for expansion and wealth. The Indian is powerless to defend himself. "The West wants to take what is left of the Indians' estate, and the rest of the country is not interested," a recent book on Indians noted.

Indians in the areas complain that their congressmen ignore them. "The Arizona delegation to Congress refuses to submit our bills," lamented Thomas A. Segundo, chairman of the Papago Tribal Council. "Pressure groups in the state work against us."

The big industries in the Western states include tourism, mining, agriculture and other forms of natural resource development. Timber interests have produced pressures for termination of the Klamath and Colville Indians in the Northwest, and have been significant in the Blue Lake controversy involving the Taos Pueblo Indians in Northern New Mexico. Uranium interests want exploration rights on Indian land, and have refused to provide anti-radiation protection to Indians whom they hire; livestock interests let their animals roam on Indian lands, paying little or nothing for grazing privileges. And in the West, where water is gold, the largest combination of economic interests relates to competition for water rights held by the Indians.

Agriculture interests want water for irrigation and land reclamation. The cities and industrial areas want water for drinking and hydroelectric power. The Indians often have a superior right, guaranteed in law, to the volume of water they possessed historically. But powerful political pressures from Congress, reaching to the Department of the Interior, have shrunk those rights. Every time an attempt is made to restore land to the Indians or place it in trust, Western political forces react against it. The land would be tax-free, and the Western states already are burdened by vast non-taxable federal holdings. These battles among local and regional interests are decided in the Interior and Insular Affairs Committees of Congress.

The leadership of these two committees exercises exceptional control over Indian affairs, in part because of the low prestige the committee holds, and in part because of the low level of seniority among its members.

The Chairman of the Senate Interior and Insular Affairs Committee, Senator Jackson of Washington, is considered a great conservationist and defense expert by his friends. (President Nixon offered him a cabinet post as Secretary of Defense.) Detractors say he is married to the aerospace industry, and call him "The Senator from Boeing."

Rep. Wayne N. Aspinall, 73-year-old chairman of the House committee, represents 35 sparsely-populated counties in Colorado's fourth district, where water can make the difference between poverty and affluence.

Water transportation in South Dakota.   JAMES FOOTE

Two other principal figures must be mentioned. Senator Clinton P. Anderson of New Mexico, chairman of the Interior Committee for two years, is still more influential than Jackson, although he gave up the chairmanship in 1963. Anderson is 74 years old, in ill health and barely able to speak, but his hard-line policies and pro-termination point of view continue to dominate the committee. Part of the reason for the enduring domination is Anderson's old staff man on the committee, James Gamble. A professional staff member since 1955, Gamble stayed on when Anderson passed the chairmanship to Jackson.

Little legislation of national interest passes through the Interior committees and so committee slots usually go to members with little or no seniority. Between 1957 and 1968, the Senate committee lost five members, and gained only two. *The large gap in seniority between the old-timers, such as Anderson, Jackson and Aspinall, and the newer members gives the leadership near absolute power.*

Senator Anderson, a former Secretary of Agriculture under Truman, is a great advocate of the National Forest Service (part of USDA) which frequently does battle with the Indians over land. Anderson's ties with banking, timber, uranium and other industrial interests in his home state of New Mexico often put him in opposition to Indian demands. Nowhere is this better illustrated than in the sensitive Blue Lake controversy in Northern New Mexico, involving the Taos Pueblo Indians (See the Holy Land Chapter).

Paul Bernal, a Taos Pueblo Indian and a leader in the fight to regain the sacred lake, related the following conversation:

> "I said to Senator Anderson: 'Just because you are a big white man and I am little, merely an Indian, does not mean that I will do what you say. No!' I said. 'My people will not sell our Blue Lake that is our church, for $10 million, and accept three thousand acres, when we know that 50,000 acres is ours. We cannot sell what is sacred. It is not ours to sell.'
> I said to Senator Anderson: 'Only God can take it

away from us. Washington is not God. The U S.
Senate is not God!'
I said to Senator Anderson: 'Why do you want to steal
our sacred land?'
Senator Anderson said: 'Paul, I like you. But there is
timber on that land, millions of dollars of timber.' " [1]

Anderson is a supporter of termination for the Indian
tribes, although that ceased to be federal policy a decade
ago. At hearings for the confirmation of BIA commissioners,
he repeatedly raises questions about the desirability of the
BIA working itself out of a job.

James Gamble is even more committed to termination.
Ralph Nader, the lawyer-writer, called Gamble ". . . the
chief congressional worker for termination of Indian reservations and assimilation of the Indian into the mainstream of
American life. The intensity of his animosity toward what he
considers the privileged position of Indians and the BIA,
which he says has a vested interest in this position, is almost
startling." [2]

Senator Jackson also favors termination. In recent years
he has worked diligently for the termination of the Colville
tribe, in Washington. It is reliably reported that Jackson and
Anderson were largely responsible for the resignation of
Philleo Nash, President Kennedy's first BIA commissioner.
Jackson was said to be angry because Nash resisted termination of the Colville Indians, whose reservation includes a
valuable timber reserve coveted by companies and the National Forest Service. [3]

The House committee, slightly less Western in its orientation, has been less enthusiastic for termination. Congressman Aspinall is no great champion of Indian interests, but
has generally taken a hands-off stance except where Indians
in Colorado are concerned. His committee voted out legislation to give the Blue Lake area to the Taos Pueblo Indians,
but the Senate buried the bill. His central concern has been
reclamation projects. In this connection, however, Aspinall
consistently sides with white farmers and irrigation and agricultural interests. So powerful are these interests, and so

expressly anti-Indian in their orientation, that in the early 1950's then-Senator McCarran of Nevada was able to have the local BIA superintendent transferred from Nevada for siding with Paiute Indians against local farmers. Congressmen from the West, working with these groups, have inserted prohibitions in appropriations bills to prevent the Paiutes from building additional irrigation projects on their land, although the Paiute land is among the more fertile areas in the West.

From the Indian's viewpoint, there is little difference between the active hostility shown by the Senate committee and the passive unconcern of Aspinall's House panel. Either way, the Indian finds himself victimized through constant demands for his land, water and other resources. The most dire threat now facing the Indian originated in the House committee: the Colorado River Basin Act. Passed by Congress in September 1968, it authorizes construction of the huge Central Arizona water diversion project and various other works in the Colorado River Basin, at a combined cost of more than $1.3 billion—the largest reclamation program ever authorized by one bill.

The Central Arizona plan provides for a 400-mile system of aqueducts, dams and other devices to divert water from the Colorado River to arid areas near Phoenix and Tucson, Arizona. The bill also authorizes five reclamation projects on Colorado's Western slope—all in Aspinall's district—at a cost of $392 million. Opposition to the bill came from Northwest congressmen, who viewed the plan as a means of importing water from two Northwest rivers, the Columbia and the Snake. They insisted on a 10-year prohibition against studies on importing water and ordered a general study of water availability. The number one advocate for the Northwest was Senator Jackson. Inclusion of the moratorium on importation studies postponed a clash brewing between Southwest and Northwest interests. As Southwest water needs become more crucial, however, pressure for importation is certain to increase.

Although no one consulted the Indians or even gave

Indian water rights much thought during debate on Aspinall's Colorado River Basin Act, the Indians claim water from all the rivers involved. Thus, no matter who wins—Southwest or Northwest—the Indian will lose. He will be the last considered, if at all. The conservationists overlook the Indian in their attempt to maintain the delicate balance of nature, while providing for the white man's needs.

Subcommittees of the Interior committees are established to provide special and continuous consideration of Indian affairs. The subcommittees are comparatively impotent, however, and tend to thwart efforts by congressmen who support needed legislation for Indians.

Unlike other congressional committees, the Subcommittees and their chairmen have surprisingly little influence in matters of benefit to the Indians. The Indian Subcommittee of the Senate Interior Committee, now chaired by Senator George McGovern of South Dakota, has had such chairmen as Lee Metcalf of Montana and Frank Church of Idaho. But their efforts to resolve the Indian heirship problem and move other legislation of benefit to the Indians met with constant frustration.

Some of the internal fighting within the subcommittee came to light in 1966, when Robert Bennett became BIA Commissioner. The full committee issued a scathing criticism of the BIA that year, written by Gamble.[4] The report called for termination of the reservations and an end to the BIA. Several members of the Indian Subcommittee were puzzled by the report, however, and doubted the wisdom of its recommendations. Senator Frank Moss of Utah and others promised a re-examination.

Some months later, after McGovern had become the subcommittee chairman, he introduced a Senate resolution expressing concern for the plight of the Indian and calling for a new policy under which "American Indian and Alaska native property will be protected [and] Indian culture and identity . . . respected. . . ." The McGovern statement called for recognition, strengthening and development of Indian communities.

Anderson and Jackson were unenthusiastic, but supported the resolution. It took nearly two years for it to be adopted. The effect of the measure was minimal, but it does illustrate the futility of seeking reform for Indians through the Senate Interior Committee. McGovern, Moss, Metcalf, Fannin and others who want to see the Indian better treated have found it more effective to outflank the Interior Committees and move through other committees concerned with poverty, education or health. *As long as the Interior Committees maintain their present jurisdictional monopoly and leadership, progress from within the committees will be effectively thwarted at the top.*

It is the leadership that sets the philosophy for the committees, and the overriding philosophy and framework within which they approach Indian problems operate to the Indians' detriment. Because the Senate committee is basically for termination, any constructive discussion of long-range goals and priorities for Indians is impossible. Even if the termination philosophy were abandoned, the Committee's tendency to consider Indian problems in the context of physical resources would rule out a whole range of considerations as not germane (except to the Indians themselves). The BIA's greatest need for expansion is in the areas of education, job training and placement, housing and industrial development. Yet the Interior committees remain preoccupied with questions of oil leases and Indian land, water and mortgage rights. Questions of tribal organization, community development and even education are ignored. In the Senate during 1967 and 1968, 90 per cent of the bills which passed through the Indian Affairs Subcommittee dealt with Indian land or land claims money.

Speaking in Santa Fe in 1966, Interior Secretary Stewart Udall noted the staleness of the committees' approach. "I'm surprised . . . how little initiative has come from Congress of new ideas, new legislation," he said. He suggested Congress, the Interior Department and the Indians should develop a closer dialogue. "Let's see if we can frame new relationships with Congress, with the Indian leaders and the

Indian people in such a way that we can achieve the result that I think everyone is agreed upon. I don't think, in terms of long-term policy, that there is any great disagreement between me and most of the members of the Congress." The leadership of the Senate Interior Committee might well disagree.

The crux of the matter is that the Indian problem is, and is not, a land problem.

Trust obligations with regard to preserving the land's tax-free status, exempting it from state regulation—these are land problems, stemming directly from treaty obligations.

Other Indian problems are land problems, too, but in a quite different sense from that which the Department of the Interior and the Congressional committees would recognize. They are land problems in the sense that one is asking: how can a people whose whole identity is defined in terms of a land base achieve economic, cultural and political self-sufficiency, using that land base in a manner which is both efficient and in harmony with their own values?

The Congressional committees and the land reclamation and water people are not sympathetic to this sort of talk. As former BIA Commissioner Nash noted in an interview, "they suffer from an understandable but just fatal defect in dealing with Indian people. They assume that the value system of the Anglo-Saxon is universal, and that the individual ownership of property is the only natural way for people to live." [5]

Thus, this statement by Senator Anderson in the 87th Congress: "By giving a preferential right to the tribe to buy [land], the tribe will gradually buy it all and you will never have individual ownership of property."

Discussion about Indians, even in terms of land, lie outside the range of considerations which the Interior committees will recognize. They can understand arguments directed to development and exploitation of the land. They can understand, even if only as a matter of political expediency, the need to create game preserves and "reservations" for birds and wildlife. But they are not responsive to a culture which

sees its relationship to the land as a natural expression of the universal kinship between things that fly, and four-leggeds and two leggeds.

The worst effect of review by the Senate and House Interior committees is to deprive the Indians of a national forum in which a consensus of good will and desire to right old wrongs can be translated into effective action. Indians have no significant voting strength, but they do enjoy broad favorable public sentiment which could be converted into political clout. The iron-fisted ways in which the committees treat Indian matters, however, nullify this support.

The special federal relationship which Indians hold gives them no strength to redress the odds which they face daily. Their struggle at the local level—the few and powerless against the many and politically potent is the same battle with the same odds when transplanted to the banks of the Potomac. Like the Interior Department, Congress becomes simply another stage on which the interests operating to oppress the Indian on the local level attain national roles.

PAUL CONKLIN

Part Four

CIVILIZING THE WHITE MAN— A TRIBUTE TO INDIAN CULTURE

"You will forgive me if I tell you that my people were Americans for thousands of years before your people were. The question is not how you can Americanize us but how we can Americanize you. We have been working at that for a long time. Sometimes we are discouraged at the results. But we will keep trying. And the first thing we want to teach you is that, in the American way of life, each man has respect for his brother's vision. Because each of us respected his brother's dream, we enjoyed freedom here in America while your people were busy killing and enslaving each other across the water. The relatives you left behind are still trying to kill each other because they have not learned there that freedom is built on my respect for my brother's vision and his respect for mine. We have a hard trail ahead of us in trying to Americanize you and your white brothers. But we are not afraid of hard trails."[1]

The white man is a newcomer to the American experiment. His roots grip just beneath the ground; the Indian's go back at least 25,000 years, to the bowels of ancient history. In the wise eyes of experience it is the white man, not the Indian, who must be civilized.

> "As the archeologists dug downward into the rocky debris [near Albuquerque] they found layers showing that generation after generation of early men had lived atop the rubble of the one before.
>
> "The bottommost layer revealed clearly the presence of early man—scraps of flint, bones of mammoths and bison that had been shattered as if to extract the marrow, charcoal deposits from fires. Among the shattered bones, the archeologists found flint knives and scrapers, presumably used for working skins, and most important, flint spear points. . . . There has been dispute about the dating of Sandia, with dates ranging between a conservative 12,000 years of age to an extreme of 25,000 years." [2]

The Indian sees himself as a member of a living culture. To be a member of a living culture is to believe that it is preferable to be what one is rather than to be something one is not.

The white man holds no patent on violence or inhumanity, but in relations with the original Americans, the occupying settlers committed many senseless atrocities.

Contrary to Hollywood's history book, it was the white man who created the tradition of scalping.

> "Whatever its exact origins, there is no doubt that [the spread of] scalp-taking . . . was due to the barbarity of white men rather than to the barbarity of red men. White settlers early offered to pay bounties on dead Indians, and scalps were actual proof of the deed. Governor Kieft of New Netherland is usually credited with originating the idea of paying for Indian scalps, as they were more convenient to handle than whole heads, and they offered the same proof that an Indian had been killed. By liberal payments for scalps, the Dutch virtually cleared southern New York and New Jersey of Indians before the English supplanted them. By 1703 the colony of Massachusetts was paying the equivalent of about $60 for every Indian scalp. In the mid-eighteenth century, Pennsylvania fixed the bounty for a male

Indian scalp at $134; a female's was worth only $50. Some white entrepreneurs simply hatcheted any old Indians that still survived in their towns." 3

The white man engaged compulsively in unnecessary slaughter—not only of the Indian but much of his life substance.

"That fall [1883], they say, the last of the bison herd was slaughtered by *Wasichus* [white man]. I can remember when the bison were so many that they could not be counted, but more and more *Wasichus* came to kill them until there were only heaps of bones scattered where they used to be. The *Wasichus* did not kill them to eat; they killed them for the metal that makes them crazy, and they took only the hides to sell. Sometimes they did not even take the hides, only the tongues; and I have heard that fireboats came down the Missouri loaded with dried bison tongues. You can see that the men who did this were crazy. . . ." 4

The Indian extended generosity to the white stranger on his continent; the white man returned the Indian's generosity with treachery and oppression.

"Once we were happy in our own country and we were seldom hungry, for then the two-leggeds and the four-leggeds lived together like relatives, and there was plenty for them and for us. But the *Wasichus* came, and they have made little islands for us and other little islands for the four-leggeds, and always these islands are becoming smaller, for around them surges the gnawing flood of the *Wasichu;* and it is dirty with lies and greed." 5

Our inhumanity extends even to our own kind.

In 1886 Black Elk, an Oglala Sioux holy man, journeyed east to Chicago and New York with a "wild west" show. He hoped to:

". . . learn some secret of the *Wasichu* [white man] that would help my people somehow. . . . I did not see anything to help my people. I could see that the *Wasichus* did not care for each other the way our people did before the nation's hoop was broken. They would take everything from each other if they

could, and so there were some who had more of
everything than they could use, while crowds of
people had nothing at all and maybe were starving.
They had forgotten that the earth was their mother.
This could not be better than the old ways of my
people. There was a prisoner's house on an island
where the big water came up to the town, and we
saw that one day. Men pointed guns at the prisoners
and made them move around like animals in a cage.
This made me feel very sad, because my people too
were penned up in islands, and maybe that was the way
the *Wasichus* were going to treat them." [6]

Much of what we are, our greatness, comes from the
Indian; not just the land, but our agricultural products, many
of our medical practices, and some of our most cherished
political traditions. Corn and potatoes, peanuts, squash, pep-
pers, tobacco, avocados—these were cultivated by the Indian
long before the white man's arrival. Many of America's
contributions to medical science, until the last few decades,
dated back to the Indians—quinine, cocaine, witch hazel,
petroleum jelly.

The Iroquois Confederacy was a model for our federal system. Canasatego, Chief of the Iroquois, advised the
Colonial governors meeting at Lancaster in 1744:

"Our Wise Forefathers established Union and Amity
between the Five Nations. This has made us formidable;
this has given us great Weight and Authority with our
neighboring Nations. We are a powerful Confederacy;
and by your observing the same Methods, our Wise
Forefathers have taken, you will acquire such Strength
and power. Therefore whatever befalls you, never fall
out with one another." [7]

Benjamin Franklin, did not miss the point. "It would be a
strange thing," he advised the Albany Congress in 1754, "if
Six Nations of ignorant savages should be capable of form-
ing a scheme for such an union, and be able to execute it
in such a manner as that it has subsisted ages and appears
indissoluble; and yet that a like union should be impractica-
ble for ten or a dozen English colonies, to whom it is more
necessary and must be more advantageous, and who cannot

be supposed to want an equal understanding of their interests." [9]

For this Indian union to be a success, however, leadership was made accountable to the people. Indian leadership understood that it could not presume to speak for all, that its authority was limited to the scope and duration of the task to be performed. As Tecumseh insisted at the chiefs' council meeting at Vincennes in 1810,

> "A few chiefs have no right to barter away hunting grounds that belong to all the Indians, for a few paltry presents or a keg or two of whiskey. . . . It requires all to make a bargain for all." [9]

The first white explorers in the West were delighted to find leaders willing to sign treaties with them. They did not understand the limitations of Indian leadership, however, and extended too much faith to the treaties. An agreement between one Shoshone leader and the whites could be made in good faith, but not be kept by another Shoshone. In the Indian's tribal form of government, no mechanism existed to force the leader's agreements on his people. [10]

Even among the wiser Americans of the time, however, understanding of the Indian and his mores ran thin. ". . . Indeed," Benjamin Franklin said, "if it be the Design of Providence to extirpate these Savages in order to make room for cultivators of the Earth, it seems not improbable that Rum may be the appointed Means. It has already annihilated all the tribes who formerly inhabited the Sea-coast." [11]

The Indian has barely survived that philosophy although he faces it as constantly today as he did in Franklin's time. And when he is not fighting for his life before a Congressional committee or a Reclamation Bureau bulldozer, the Indian still contributes to society. In May, 1969, a previously unknown Kiowa named N. Scott Momaday became the first Indian to win a Pulitzer Prize for his novel *House Made of Dawn.*

> *"There was a house made of dawn. It was made of pollen and of rain, and the land was very old and everlasting. There were many colors on the hills, and*

the plain was bright with different-colored clays and sands. Red and blue and spotted horses grazed in the plain, and there was a dark wilderness on the mountains beyond. The land was still and strong. It was beautiful all around." [12]

That the surviving Indian is still apart and unique is a tribute to his tenacity. If nothing else, he has proven expert at defending himself against efforts to "civilize" and change him. A BIA official told with exasperation how members of the Sac and Fox tribes at Tama, Iowa held technical jobs in the aircraft industry of the cities but returned to the reservation and their tribal ways on weekends. It is Indianness that comes first, and that is why the Sac and Fox have fought for

A Mandan woman with her grandchild.   ED ECKSTEIN

control of their schools; they want their heritage retained and their language taught.

> "The Mesquakie language, our ways, our religion are interwoven into one. All are significant to our religion. With another language we cannot perform our religion. This is taught right from the beginning." [13]

Indianness—being an Indian in spirit and in blood—means a refusal to become extinct.

> *"You have brought me down the white road.*
> *There in mid-earth you have placed me.*
> *I shall stand erect upon the earth." [14]*

And so he fights to keep his heritage and move ahead in the white man's world as well. The Tlingits put outboard motors on their canoes. The Indians of the West wear Levis, not buckskin. Provided there is a need and an opportunity, the Indian will adapt in ways which do not destroy the familiar, and perhaps more sane rhythm of life that they have known. The Yankton Sioux have no clock in their electronic components factory. In New Mexico, White Mountain Apaches live in straw huts called Wickiups, but also run tourist facilities, gas stations, motels, and a prosperous co-operative cattle ranching business.

The Indian has not resisted our technology, only enslavement by technology:

> *"We shall learn all these devices the White Man has.*
> *We shall handle his tools for ourselves.*
> *We shall master his machinery, his inventions,*
> *his skills, his medicine,*
> *his planning;*
> *But we'll retain our beauty*
> *And still be Indian." [15]*

The Indian knows the white man's world, but the Indian world, to the white man, remains a mystery. Yet the Indian world offers so much, offers Indian solutions to white man's problems.

There are Indian voices that speak to each of our society's present problems:

The Sense of Personal Isolation

"Your dead cease to love you and the land of their nativity as soon as they pass the portals of the tomb and wander way beyond the stars. They soon are forgotten and never return. Our dead never forget the beautiful world that gave them being." [16]

International Relations

"The changes of fortune and vicissitudes of war made you my conqueror. When my last resources were exhausted, my warriors, worn down with long and toilsome marches, yielded, and I became your prisoner. . . . I am now an obscure member of a nation that formerly honored and respected my opinions. The pathway to glory is rough, and many gloomy hours obscure it. May the Great Spirit shed light on yours, and that you may never experience the humiliation that the power of the American government has reduced me to, is the wish of him who, in his native forests, was once as proud as you."

—Chief Black Hawk 1832 [17]

Crime

"You have a very complicated legal system. It is not that way with my people. I have always thought that you had so many laws because you were a lawless people. Why else would you need so many laws? After all, Europe opened all prisons and penitentiaries and sent all their criminals to this country. Perhaps that is why you need so many laws. I hope we never have to reach such an advanced state of civilization." [18]

Group sanctions, community ostracism, and disapproval are the Indian alternatives. Thomas Jefferson was moved to observe that perhaps, judging by results, the Indian system for maintaining law and order was superior:

"Imperfect as this species of coercion may seem, *crimes are very rare among them* [the Indians of Virginia]; insomuch that were it made a question, whether no law, as among the savage Americans, or too much law, as among the civilized Europeans, submits man to the greatest evil, one who has seen both conditions of existence would pronounce it to be the last; and that the sheep are happier of themselves, than under care of the wolves. It will be said, the great societies cannot exist without government. The savages, therefore, break them into small ones." [19] (emphasis added)

The Indian's wisdom, still embodied in tribal codes today, is that there is a limitation to the effectiveness of force, criminal punishment and prison sentences as a solution to problems of law and order. The Indians rely more on group pressure and disapproval. They shift law enforcement from the courts to other forums equally as legitimate:

"In Alaska . . . all disputes except murder are settled by a song duel. . . . The song duel consists of lampoons, insults, and obscenities that the disputants sing to each other and of course, to their delighted audience. . . . The loser suffers a great punishment, for disapproval of the community is very difficult to bear in a group as small as that of the Eskimo." [20]

An impersonal legal system, separated from local communities and neighborhood participation and legitimation, perpetuates itself in this country. A comparison, such as the legal scholar Felix Cohen has made, brings out the impersonal sterility of our own ways of coping with law breakers:

"The form of punishment is, typically, forced labor for the benefit of the tribe or of the victim of the offense, rather than imprisonment.

"The tribal penal codes, for the most part, do not contain the usual catch-all provisions to be found in state penal codes (vagrancy, conspiracy, criminal syndicalism, etc.), under which almost any unpopular individual may be convicted of crime. . . .

"The comparison suggests that perhaps the Indian penal codes may be more 'civilized' than the non-Indian." [21] (emphasis added)

A Sense of Community

The Indian has a strong sense of community. The white man still lives by the Poor Laws of England.

"An Eskimo praises a hunter for the way he hurled the harpoon but not for the way he shared the meat from the seal the harpoon killed. Sharing is a kinsman's due, and it is not the category of a gift. The Arctic explorer Peter Freuchen once made the mistake of thanking an Eskimo hunter, with whom he had been living, for some meat. Freuchen's bad manners were promptly corrected: 'You must not thank for your meat; it is your right to get parts. In this country, nobody wishes to be dependent upon others. . . . With gifts you make slaves just as with whips you make dogs!' "[22]

Our isolation—from past, present and future was summed up by one Indian: "You are each a one-man tribe." If there is a special characteristic of Indian culture that begins to emerge, it is the vitality of that sense of community which beggars description and defies the probing analytical mind of the dissecting social scientist.

One of the few white men to grasp this truth, to understand the irrelevance of his scientific methodology, records his voyage of discovery:

"Administering my questionnaire within Cherokee households was an unforgettable ordeal, for myself and for Cherokees. This was not so because Cherokees were hostile, or reluctant to answer. . . . Where whites, especially if on welfare, might be evasive when asked the source and amount of their income, Cherokees were precise. What tormented Cherokees, and myself more, was that the questions simply did not fit Cherokee experience. They were all but unanswerable. . . .

"Eventually I realized that *all* Cherokee are kin, though many are unacquainted, and that Cherokees are not consciously aware of their 'kinship system' because each particular relationship between kin acquires its own meaning in face to face interaction. . . . It finally dawned on me that this is how Cherokees live—as people born in permanent and fixed relation, who come and go, sharing resources and supporting one another. Wherever he might live, a Cherokee is part of an on-going group of relatives. Cherokees do not experience themselves as separate from these relatives nor do the activities we categorize as 'visiting', 'helping', 'lending', etc., define their relatedness." [23]

In the process of securing the blessings of a scientific urban civilization, we have destroyed many of the bonds which knit people together. We have ignored a living culture which warns of the ultimate interdependence of all living beings and all matter.

The Indian accepts the inevitability of change for it is the one constant he has known. The future can bring him no worse vicissitudes.

> *"Man came down the ladder to the plain a long time ago. It was a slow migration, though he came only from the caves in the canyons and the tops of the mesas nearby. There are low, broken walls on the table tops and smoke-blackened caves in the cliffs, where still there are metates and broken bowls and ancient ears of corn, as if the prehistoric civilization had gone out among the hills for a little while and would return; and then everything would be restored to an older age, and time would have returned upon itself and a bad dream of invasion and change would have been dissolved in an hour before the dawn. For man, too, has tenure in the land; he dwelt upon the land twenty-five thousand years ago, and his gods before him.*
>
> *"The people of the town have little need. They do not hanker after progress and have never changed their essential way of life. Their invaders were a long time in conquering them; and now, after four centuries of Christianity, they still pray in Tanoan to the old deities of the earth and sky and make their living from the things that are and have always been within their reach; while in the discrimination of pride they acquire from their conquerors only the luxury of example. They have assumed the names and gestures of their enemies, but have held on to their own, secret souls; and in this there is a resistance and an overcoming, a long outwaiting."*

> *House Made of Dawn*

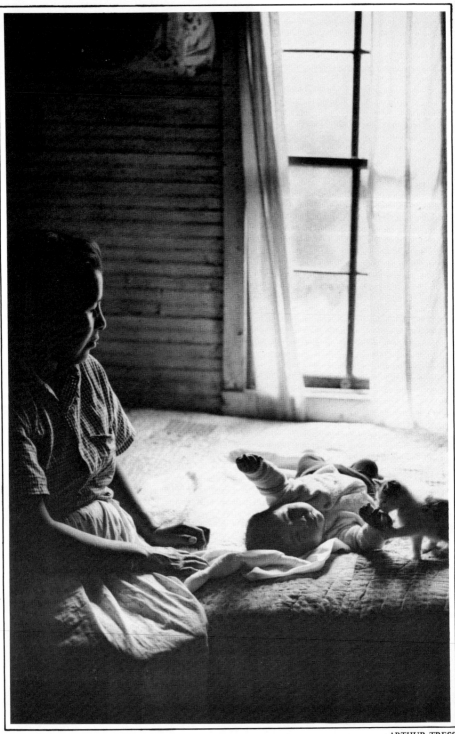

ARTHUR TRESS

POSTSCRIPT

Where Do We Go From Here?

A REPORT WITHOUT RECOMMENDATIONS

The American Indian lives in a total, closed world. This book has attempted to provide an insight into the frustrations of that world, which thwarts and penalizes individual and tribal self-realization, which rewards and perpetuates dependency, and which demands alienation from one's heritage as a price for survival. It has presented a non-Indian view, although Indians have participated at every step in compiling *Our Brother's Keeper*. It has attempted to speak to a non-Indian reader; the Indian needs no such description: he lives in that world.

No attempt has been made to unlock every door in the Bureau of Indian Affairs' domain. Libraries of official Washington have become crowded morgues for reports which document that Indians are denied basic civil rights, such as the right to counsel; that Indian welfare payments and services are grossly inadequate; that many Indians go hungry; that Indian housing is a travesty—70 per cent of it substandard; that job-training programs are insufficient, misguided and ineffective; that the relocated Indian, far from raising his living standards, is drowning anonymously in the worst ghettoes of our land. We have only touched upon each of these areas because they spring from a larger, more fundamental finding which we did not want to bury in tedious detail—that Our Brother's Keeper has fabricated an artificial world for the Indian—a world that degrades, alienates and destroys him.

The Citizens' Advocate Center does not offer recom-

*mendations. We offer this observation: that the Indians do
not need one more white man's plan for their betterment.*
Thousands of recommendations are on the shelves and in
the files, probing every corner of Indian life, every facet of
Government policy. Each calls for reorganization, shuffling
of priorities, new vistas. Among the better known:

1928—The Meriam Report consisted of 800 pages of
detailed, documented instances of injustice and neglect; 35
pages of suggested remedies including economic development, shifting away from boarding schools, respect for Indian culture, new sources of credit, a plan for a modified
form of tribal self-government. The report generated the Indian Reorganization Act of 1934, the New Deal for the
Indian, which ended with the coming of World War II.

1949—The Hoover Commission compiled a massive
volume, emphasizing self-reliance and formulating the policy
of termination for the trust status of Indian lands. It advocated shifting responsibility for Indian affairs to the states
and total assimilation for the Indian at an accelerated pace.
The Eisenhower Administration made termination the policy of the 1950's.

1961—The Secretary of the Interior, Stewart Udall's
Task Force released 67 pages of recommendations, reflecting
a cautious shift away from termination.

1961—The Commission on the Rights, Liberties and
Responsibilities of the American Indian, a private group,
published *The Indian: America's Unfinished Business*; 236
pages of detailed recommendations governing every major
phase of federal policy. It is still timely, with recommendations which stem from the basic philosophy of the Indian
Reorganization Act, the New Deal, and a conclusion that
the policies of the 1950's were disastrous.

1961—The Declaration of Indian Purpose. A wholly
ignored set of recommendations by the Indians themselves,
it too rejected the termination policy and suggested Indians
be allowed to participate "in developing their own programs
with help and guidance as needed and requested from a
local, decentralized staff. . . ."

1966—The Johnson Presidential Task Force on the American Indian. This report was highly critical of the BIA and demanded drastic reorganization from top to bottom. But the Johnson Administration suppressed it.

1967—The Indian Resource Development Act (better known as the "Omnibus Bill" for Indians) and reports accompanying it in Congress ranged over major areas of Indian policy but focused on economic development and sources of credit. It lacked emphasis on self-determination and was widely opposed by Indians who, rightly or not, feared it meant termination in a new form. The act never passed.

1967—Report of the Inter-Agency Task Force of 1967, produced by representatives of the Interior Department, the Bureau of the Budget and the Office of Economic Opportunity. It provided a watered-down set of recommendations which were incorporated into President Johnson's Indian message to Congress of March 6, 1968. The report called for "self-determination rather than termination," but fell far short of the massive therapy and funding which the Presidential Task Force considered mandatory.

1969—The American Indian and the Bureau of Indian Affairs—1969, prepared by Alvin M. Josephy, Jr. at the request of the incoming Nixon Administration. A scholarly and candid study by a leading student of Indian affairs, it focused critically on the BIA structure and suggested removing it from the Interior Department, creating an Indian Agency within the Executive office, and extensive structural changes.

With the exception of those proposals stemming from termination, a policy which the Nixon Administration has disavowed, the major policy objectives of each of these proposals, stretching over 41 years, have remained constant. Their main thrust can be summarized:

1. Termination shall take place only with Indian consent; the trust status of Indians lands must be inviolate.

2. Indian culture must be respected, with the Indians
   left to decide the degree of white man's culture
   which they wish to absorb.
3. Indian education must be radically improved—
   boarding schools phased out and replaced with reservation day schools; public schools serving Indians
   under federal grants should be required to meet
   their special needs; locally elected school boards and
   parent participation should be encouraged.
4. Heirship land ownership which produces fractionali-
   zation of Indian land holdings must be reversed.
   Lands should be voluntarily consolidated with title
   held by the tribe, where desired.
5. Economic development and Indian job opportunities
   must be expanded.
6. The BIA must be reorganized, even taken out of
   Interior, and given more independence.
7. Indians must be provided with institutions through
   which they can participate and come to determine
   their own lives.

In a separately-bound document we have prepared a
condensed analysis of past recommendations for use by Indians as well as other interested parties who seek to devise
solutions. Government policy, practice, organization and
philosophy must be substantially changed—but there is no
need to reinvent the wheel.

*Recommendations have come to have a special non-
meaning for Indians. They are part of a tradition in which
policy and programs are dictated by non-Indians, even when
dialogue and consultation have been promised.*

Dialogue and consultation have served the Indians
poorly. Every treaty they have signed, it is said, came only
after mutual negotiation and dialogue. Nevertheless, that
dialogue involved a defeated nation and a conquerer—and
more recent consultations have carried the same flavor.

In the same style, unilateral renunciations of past obligations have been camouflaged by promises from the Government to proceed only with the consent of the Indians. But

consent has been involuntary, and the dialogue has been fraudulent.

Indians were assured in the early 1950's that no termination action would be taken without careful consultation. BIA Commissioner Glen L. Emmons, the father of termination, said repeatedly: ". . . I can and do pledge that each tribal group will be fully consulted by the Bureau of Indian Affairs before we take any final action recommending a termination program to the Congress."

President Eisenhower made the same promise. Emmons, his appointee, gave a long discourse on the semantics of "consultation," to assure that he meant much more than merely advising the Indians.

The promises were broken. The Indians were consulted infrequently, and when they were sought out they were coerced with threats to freeze claims awards, promises of extra concessions and a variety of high pressure tactics which effectively shot down any meaningful Indian participation or opposition. Hearings on termination became a *pro forma* orchestration of decisions already made in Washington, by non-Indians.

But the Indian need not go back to the Eisenhower years for proof that Government cannot be trusted. In 1966 the Indian was promised that he would be centrally involved in the creation of a master plan for Indians—the Johnson Administration Indian Resource Development Act—which was introduced in Congress a year later. The Interior Department wrote the bill, and Indian support was viewed as crucial for its passage. Regional hearings were held in nine areas, with Indians participating and offering a total of 1,950 recommendations. Only later did they learn that the legislation already had been drafted—before the hearings. The bill failed.

At some point the cycle must stop. Pre-packaged proposals and consultation that is merely rubber-stamp ratification can never bring acceptable approaches to solving the Indian problems. History, if it has taught anything, should demonstrate that unless the Indians can shape their own poli-

cies and priorities and have the opportunity to participate—
an opportunity which is, after all, integral to American
democracy—the solutions will fail.

To be sure, it is easier for government to do it all. It is
much easier for well-meaning non-Indians to lay out obvious
improvements for on and off the reservations, and ask the
Indian to agree. The Government has, historically, suc-
cumbed to the easy way out.

Except for the *Declaration of Indian Purpose,* all
major studies and recommendations have been conceived,
executed and promoted by non-Indians. And yet only the
Indians have a persistent interest in change and improvement. For the rest of the nation, it is merely a nagging matter of conscience.

The Citizens' Advocate Center will offer no recommendations. Instead we offer to work with—but outside the
framework of—a representative Indian organization in a
problem-solving process which parts with past tradition,
which places all initiative in Indian hands and which broadens
the opportunity for continuous participation by Indians in
shaping their own destinies. This does not require recommendations. It requires action—a process which will bring
in Indian youths, who constitute more than half of the population, tribal leaders, respected individuals in the Indian community, the never-consulted organizations, and others.

The Declaration of the Five County Cherokees said
long ago:

> *"Now, we shall not rest until we have regained our
> rightful place. We shall tell our young people what we
> know. We shall send them to the corners of the earth to
> learn more. They shall lead us.*
>
> *"Now we have much to do. When our task is done, we
> will be ready to rest.*
>
> *"In these days, intruders, named without our consent,
> speak for the Cherokees. When the Cherokee govern-
> ment is the Cherokee people, we shall rest.*
>
> *"In these days, the high courts of the United States
> listen to people who have been wronged. When our*

wrongs have been judged in these courts, and the illegalities of the past have been corrected, we shall rest.

"In these days, there are countless ways by which people make their grievances known to all Americans. When we have learned these new ways that bring strength and power, and we have used them, we shall rest.

"In these days, we are losing our homes and our children's homes. When our homeland is protected, for ourselves and for the generations to follow, we shall rest.

"In the vision, of our creator, we declare ourselves ready to stand proudly among the nationalities of these United States of America."

So be it.

Photographs on pages 41 and 113 by Ed Eckstein.

Paperback cover and dust jacket based upon an original by Patricia Benson.

SELECT BIBLIOGRAPHY

A Free Choice Program for American Indians, Report of the President's Task Force on American Indians, December, 1966.

ANDRIST, RALPH K., *The Long Death*, New York, Collier-Macmillon, Ltd., 1964.

BACHRACH, WILLIAM, "An Assault in the Sixties," *The Humanist*, pp. 183-184, September, 1967

BENNETT, ROBERT L., Indian Leaders Conference on the proposed "Omnibus Bill," Department of Interior, October-December, 1966.

COHEN, FELIX, "Indian Rights and the Federal Courts," *Minnesota Law Review*, Vol. 24, 1940.

COHEN, LUCY KRAMER, ed., *The Legal Conscience: Selected Papers of Felix S. Cohen;* New Haven, Yale Univ. Press, 1960.

COHEN, WARREN H., and MAUSE, PHILIP L., "The Indian: The Forgotten American," *Harvard Law Review*, Vol. 81, No. 8, p. 1820, June, 1968.

COMPTROLLER GENERAL OF THE UNITED STATES, *Report to the Congress: Improvements Achieved by the Bureau of Indian Affairs in the Management of Supplies,* 1968.

COMPTROLLER GENERAL OF THE UNITED STATES, *Report to the Congress: More Precise Planning Initiated in Employee Housing Construction Program, Bureau of Indian Affairs, Department of the Interior,* 1968.

COMPTROLLER GENERAL OF THE UNITED STATES, *Report to the Congress: Need to Improve System for Managing Capitalized Equipment in the Bureau of Indian Affairs,* 1968.

COMPTROLLER GENERAL OF THE UNITED STATES, *Report to the Congress: Proposals for Improving the System for Management of Repairs and Maintenance of Buildings and Utilities,* 1968.

EMBRY, CARLOS B., *America's Concentration Camps*, New York, David McKay Co., Inc., 1956.

FARB, PETER, *Man's Rise to Civilization as Shown by the Indians of North America*, New York, E. P. Dutton and Co., Inc., 1968.

FORBES, JACK D., ed., *The Indian in America's Past*, Englewood, N. J., Prentice Hall, 1964.

HENNINGER, DANIEL and ESPOSITO, NANCY, "Regimented Non-Education: Indian Schools," *The New Republic*, pp. 18-21, February 15, 1969.

HOUGH, HENRY W., *Development of Indian Resources*, Denver, World Press, 1967.

HYDE, PHILIP, and JETT, STEPHEN C., ed., *Navajo Wildlands: As Long as the Rivers Shall Run,* Paterson, N.J., Sierra Club Books, 1967.

Indian Reorganization Act, 73rd Congress, 2nd Session, June 18, 1934.

JOSEPHY, JR., ALVIN M., *The American Indian and the Bureau of Indian Affairs—1969: A Study with Recommendations,* February 10, 1969.

JOSEPHY, *The Indian Heritage of America,* New York, Alfred A. Knopf, Inc., 1968.

KOCH, ADRIENNE, and PEDEN, WILLIAM, ed., *The Life and Selected Writings of Thomas Jefferson,* New York, Random House, 1944.

LABAREE, LEONARD W., ed., *et. al., The Autobiography of Benjamin Franklin,* New Haven, Yale University Press, 1964.

MOMADAY, N. SCOTT, *House Made of Dawn, New York,* Harper, 1968.

NADER, RALPH, "Lo, The Poor Indian," *The New Republic,* pp. 14-15, March 30, 1968.

NATIONAL CONGRESS OF AMERICAN INDIANS, *Position Paper: Indian Views on the Reorganization of the Bureau of Indian Affairs,* Albuquerque, New Mexico, May 6, 1969.

ORFIELD, GARY, *A Study of the Termination Policy,* Chicago, University of Chicago, 1966.

Report to the Secretary of the Interior by the Task Force on Indian Affairs, July 10, 1961.

STEINER, STAN, *The New Indians,* New York, Harper and Row, 1968.

The Indian: America's Unfinished Business, Report of the Commission on the Rights, Liberties, and Responsibilities of the American Indian. Comp. by William A. Brophy and Sophie D. Aberle. Norman, Oklahoma, 1966.

The Problem of Indian Administration, Report of a survey made at the request of the Honorable Huber Work, Secretary of Interior, and submitted to him, John Hopkins Press, February 21, 1928.

The Voice of the American Indian: Declaration of Indian Purpose, The American Indian Chicago Conference, Chicago, 1961.

THOMAS, ROBERT K., "Powerless Politics," *New University Thought,* Vol. 4, p. 51, 1967.

"Weekly Report," *The Congressional Quarterly,* Vol. XXV, No. 21, p. 889, May 26, 1967.

UDALL, STEWART, *The Quiet Crisis,* New York, Holt, Rinehart and Winston, 1963.

NOTES AND SOURCES

PIECES OF A PUZZLE

1. Letter from Howard Kahn to Enos Poorbear, President, Oglala Sioux Tribal Council, May 16, 1968. Marshall Kaplan, Gans, and Kahn, "Description of Pine Ridge," *Oglala Sioux Model Reservation Program: The Development Potential of the Pine Ridge Indian Reservation*, p. 4, 1968.

2. "Haskell Students Face Discrimination," *The University Daily Kansan*, December 13, 1968.

THE INDIAN AND HIS KEEPERS

1. Robert K. Thomas, "Powerless Politics," *New University Thought*, Vol. 4, p. 51, 1967.

2. Warren H. Cohen, Philip L. Manle, "The Indian: The Forgotten American," *Harvard Law Review*, Vol. 81, No. 8, p. 1820, June 1968.

3. *U.S. v. Creek Nation*, 295 U.S. 103, 110 (1935); 25 C.F.R. 151.1 *et seq.* (1968); 25 U.S.C. §§ 415, 415 (c) (1964); 25 C.F.R. §§ 131.5 (a); 25 C.F.R. § 131.2; 25 C.F.R. §§ 131.14; 25 C.F.R. §§ 141.7 (1968); 25 U.S.C. § 373 (1964).

4. 25 U.S.C. § 292 (1964).

5. Lucy Kramer Cohen, ed., *The Legal Conscience: Selected Papers of Felix S. Cohen*, pp. 331-333.

6. Philip Hyde and Stephen C. Jett, ed., *Navajo Wildlands: As Long as the Rivers Shall Run.*

THE BIA: THE LESSER OF TWO EVILS

1. Statement by Earl Old Person, Chairman of Blackfeet Tribe, in testimony before Indian Leaders Conference. Bureau of Indian Affairs, Spokane, Washington, pp. 15-16, October 17-19, 1966.

2. "The Status of the Termination of the Menominee Indian Tribe," *A Report to the Committee on Appropriations, House of Representatives by the Department of the Interior, Bureau of Indian Affairs,* February 1965; CAC telephone interview with Wisconsin State Welfare Office, June 11, 1969.

3. Gary Orfield, *A Study of the Termination Policy,* pp. 15, 23.

4. *Hearings on the Education of Indian Children before a Special Subcommittee on Indian Education of the Senate Committee on Labor and Public Welfare,* 90 Cong., 1st and 2nd sess., Part V, p. 2160, October 1, 1968.

5. Statement by Rex Lee, Assistant Commissioner of Indian Affairs. *Joint Hearings on the Termination of Federal Supervision over Certain Tribes of Indians,* 83rd Cong., 2nd sess., Part VI, p. 610, quoted in William A. Brophy and Sophie D. Aberle, *The Indian: America's Unfinished Business,* p. 200, 1966.

6. Testimony by Robert L. Bennett, Commissioner, Bureau of Indian Affairs. *Hearings before the Subcommittee on Indian Affairs of the Senate Committee on Interior and Insular Affairs,* 90 Cong. 1 sess., pp. 25, 27, June 8, 1967.

7. "Weekly Report," *The Congressional Quarterly,* Vol. XXV, No. 21, p. 889, May 26, 1967.

8. Alvin M. Josephy, Jr., *The American Indian and the Bureau of Indian Affairs—1969: A Study with Recommendations,* p. 5, February 1969.

EDUCATION

1. *Hearings Before a Special Subcommittee on Indian Education of the Senate Committee on Labor and Public Welfare,* 90 Cong., 1 and 2 sess., Part I, p. 242, January 4, 1968.

2. Statement by Dr. Daniel J. O'Connell, Executive Secretary, National Committee on Mental Health. Indian Education Subcommittee Hearings, 90 Cong. 1 and 2 sess., Part I, p. 53, December 14, 1967. See also Dr. Robert L. Bergman, "A Second Report on the Problems of Boarding Schools," reprinted in the Indian Education Subcommittee Hearings, Part III, p. 1130, March 30, 1968.

3. Statement by Dr. Robert L. Leon, M.D., Professor and Chairman of the Department of Psychiatry, University of Texas Medical School. Indian Education Subcommittee Hearings 90 Cong., 1 and 2 sess., Part V, p. 2152, October 1, 1968.

4. Letter from a boarding school teacher to the late Senator Robert F. Kennedy, Chairman, Indian Education Subcommittee. Indian Education Subcommittee Hearings, 90 Cong., 1 and 2 sess., Part III, p. 1118, March 20, 1968.

5. James Coleman, "Equality of Education Opportunity," quoted by Senator Robert F. Kennedy at Indian Education Subcommittee Hearings, 90 Cong., 1 and 2 sess., Part I, p. 5, December 14, 1967; Abt Associates, Inc., *Systems Analysis Program Development and Cost-Effectiveness Modeling of Indian Education for the Bureau of Indian Affairs,* Sixth Monthly Progress Report, p. 11, December 14, 1967.

6. Brewton Berry, "The Education of American Indians: A Survey of the Literature," prepared for the Indian Education Subcommittee of the Senate Committee on Labor and Public Welfare, 91 Cong., 1 sess., p. 17.

7. Letter from a boarding school teacher to the late Senator Robert F. Kennedy, p. 118.

8. Dr. Robert L. Bergman, "Boarding Schools and Psychological Problems of Indian Children," reprinted in Indian Education Subcommittee Hearings, 90 Cong., 1 and 2 sess., Part IV, p. 1122, April 16, 1968.

9. Murray L. Wax, et al, "Formal Education in an American Indian Community," *Social Problems,* Vol. 11, No. 4, Spring 1964, reprinted in Indian Education Subcommittee Hearings, 90 Cong., 1 and 2 sess., Part IV, pp. 1391, 1403, April 16, 1968.

10. Statement by Dr. Alfonso Ortiz, Anthropologist, Princeton University. Indian Education Subcommittee Hearings of the 90 Cong., 1 and 2 sess., Part I, p. 64, December 14, 1967.

11. Statement by Rupert Costo. Indian Education Subcommittee Hearings of the 90 Cong., 1 and 2 sess., Part I, p. 242, January 4, 1968.

12. Statement by David Risling, Jr. Indian Education Subcommittee Hearings of the 90 Cong., 1 and 2 sess., Part I, p. 240, January 4, 1968.

13. Quoted by Senator Walter F. Mondale of Minnesota. Indian Education Subcommittee Hearings of the 90 Cong., 1 and 2 sess., Part V, p. 2133, October 1, 1968.

14. Statement by Mrs. Iola Hayden, Director, Oklahomans for Indian Opportunity. Indian Education Subcommittee Hearings, of the 90 Cong., 1 and 2 sess., Part II, p. 587, February 19, 1968.

15. Statement by Louis R. Gourd, Cherokee Indian, Tahlequah, Oklahoma. Indian Education Subcommittee Hearings of the 90 Cong., 1 and 2 sess., Part II, p. 547, February 19, 1968.

16. Bergman, p. 1122.

17. Official release of testimony to be given by William Pensoneau, Vice President, National Indian Youth Council at Indian Education Subcommittee Hearings of the 90 Cong., 1 and 2 sess., February 24, 1968.

18. Wax, op. cit., p. 1397.

19. Robert V. Dumont, Jr. and Murray L. Wax, The Cherokee School Society and the Intercultural Classroom, reprinted in Indian Education Subcommittee Hearings, 90 Cong., 1 and 2 sess., Part II, p. 890, February 19, 1968.

20. Wax, op. cit., p. 1420.

21. Statement by Lower Brule Sioux Tribe, Lower Brule, South Dakota. Indian Education Subcommittee Hearings before the 90 Cong. 1 and 2 sess., Part I, p. 64, December 14, 1967.

22. Letter from employee of Intermountain School to the Citizens Advocate Center, March 2, 1969.

23. Statement by Robert Costo. Indian Education Subcommittee Hearings of the 90th Con., 1 and 2 sess., Part I, p. 243, January 4, 1968.

24. Statement by Dr. Alfonso Ortiz, Anthropologist, Princeton University. Indian Education Subcommittee Hearings of the 90 Cong., 1 and 2 sess., Part I, p. 64, December 14, 1967.

25. Ibid., p. 65.

26. Statement by Fr. John Bryde, S. J., Ph.D., Superintendent, Holy Rosary Mission School, Pine Ridge, South Dakota. Indian Education Subcommittee Hearings of the 90 Cong., 1 and 2 sess., Part I, p. 45, December 14, 1967.

27. William H. Kelly, A Study of Southern Arizona School-Age Indian Children, 1966-1967, reprinted in Indian Education Subcommittee Hearings, 90 Cong., 1 and 2 sess., Part III, pp. 1105-1107, March 30, 1968.

28. "You're No Indian—You Talk Too Much," Northwest Sunday Oregonian Magazine, November 24, 1968.

29. Statement by Wilfred Antell, Minnesota Department of Education. Indian Education Subcommittee Hearings, 90 Cong., 1

and 2 sess., p. 187, February 19, 1968.

30. Wax, *op. cit.,* p. 1391.

31. Rosalie H. Wax, "The Warrior Reports," *Transaction,* May 1967, reprinted in Indian Education Subcommittee Hearings, 90 Cong., 1 and 2 sess., Part IV, p. 1304, April 16, 1968.

32. Quote by John Belindo, Executive Director, National Congress of American Indians. Indian Education Subcommittee Hearings of the 90 Cong., 1 and 2 sess., Part I, pp. 221-22, December 15, 1967.

33. Anonymous, *Education.* A theme paper written for an English class at Arizona State University.

34. Wax, "Formal Education in an American Indian Community," pp. 1379-81.

35. "Investigative Report for House Appropriations Subcommittee," Hearings on the Department of the Interior and Related Agencies Appropriations for 1969 before a Subcommittee of the House Committee on Appropriations, 90 Cong., 2 sess., p. 591, February 29, 1968.

36. Comptroller General of the United States, *Report to the Congress: More Precise Planning Initiated in Employee Housing Construction Program, Bureau of Indian Affairs, Department of the Interior,* 1968.

37. Comptroller General of the United States, *Report to the Congress: Improvements Achieved by the Bureau of Indian Affairs in the Management of Supplies,* 1968.

38. Comptroller General of the United States, *Report to the Congress: Need to Improve System for Managing Capitalized Equipment in the Bureau of Indian Affairs,* 1968.

39. Comptroller General of the United States, *Report to the Congress: Proposals for Improving the System for Management of Repairs and Maintenance of Buildings and Utilities,* 1968.

40. Letter from a boarding school teacher to Senator Robert F. Kennedy, *op. cit.*

41. Statement by Domingo Montoya, Member, National Indian Education Advisory Committee. Indian Education Subcommittee Hearings, 90 Cong., 1 and 2 sess., Part I, p. 94, December 14, 1967.

42. Statement by Robert A. Roessel, Jr., Director, Rough Rock Demonstration School, Chinle, Arizona. Indian Education Subcommittee Hearings, 90 Cong., 1 and 2 sess., Part I, p. 13, December 14, 1967.

HEALTH

1. U.S. Department of Health, Education, and Welfare, *Justifications of Appropriation Estimates for Committee on Appropriations,* Fiscal Year 1970, p. 3.

2. Marshall Kaplan, Gans, and Kahn, p. 191.

3. "Ear Doctor, Team From D.C. To Treat Eskimo Children," *Washington Star,* June 29, 1968.

4. National Commission on Community Health Services, *Health is a Community Affair,* quoted in U.S. Department of Health, Education and Welfare, Public Health Service, Division of Indian Health, Staff Paper, "Making Health Resources Available to All Beneficiaries," p. 9, January 5, 1967.

5. Marshall Kaplan, Gans, and Kahn, p. 188.

6. "Making Health Resources Available to All Beneficiaries," U.S. Department of Health, Education, and Welfare, Public Health Service, Division of Indian Health Staff Paper, pp. 5-6, January 5, 1969.

7. *Hearings on the Department of the Interior and Related Agencies Appropriations for 1969.* Interior Appropriations Subcommittee of the House Committee on Appropriations, 90 Cong., 2 Sess., Part III, pp. 502-503.

8. Annie D. Wauneka, "Helping a People to Understand," available from the Nursing Advisory Service of the National Tuberculosis Association.

9. *Ibid.*

10. *Ibid.*

11. Statement by C. J. Wagner, former Chief, Division of Indian Health, U.S. Department of Health, Education, and Welfare, Public Health Service. Third National Conference on Indian Health of the Association on American Indian Affairs, p. 31, November 19, 1964.

12. Carl E. Mindell, "Poverty, Mental Health and the Sioux," a paper presented September 19, 1968 at the South Dakota Welfare, Health and Rehabilitation Conference at Yankton, South Dakota, quoted in *Hearings on the Education of Indian Children before a Special Subcommittee on Indian Education of the Senate Committee on Labor and Public Welfare,* 90 Cong., 1 and 2 sess., Part IV, pp. 1896-97, April 16, 1968.

LAND AS SUSTENANCE AND INCOME

1. Dave Jackson, President, Quinault Tribe, Seattle Proceedings of the Annual Meeting of the American Anthropological Association, pp. 64-65, December 1, 1968.

2. Statement by the Makah Indian Tribe at *Hearings on Indian Fishing Rights before the Subcommittee on Indian Affairs of the Senate Committee on Interior and Insular Affairs,* 88 Cong., 2 sess., p. 80.

3. Statement by Gardner Brown, Economist at the University of Washington, Seattle Proceedings of the Annual Meeting of the American Anthropological Association, p. 9, December 1, 1968.

4. Statement in Seattle Proceedings of the Annual Meeting of the American Anthropological Association, p. 9, December 1, 1968.

5. "How White Traders Rob the Red Man," *Eureka Times-Standard,* November 19, 1967.

6. 25 C.F.R. § 251.22.

7. Testimony at *Hearings on the Department of the Interior and Related Agencies Appropriations for 1969 before the Interior Appropriations Subcommittee of the House Committee on Appropriations* 90 Cong., 2 sess., Part II, p. 766, February 29, 1968.

8. Henry W. Hough, *Development of Indian Resources,* p. 47.

9. Interview between John Vaninetti, Bureau of Indian Affairs Realty Officer, Fort Hall Reservation, and Citizens Advocate Center, December 6, 1968.

10. *Ibid.*

11. Letter from Mary Cornelius, Tribal Chairman, Little Shell Tribe, to Citizens Advocate Center, December 17, 1968.

12. Citizens Advocate Center Investigative Report, *Report on*

Osage County, p. 7, October 1, 1968.

13. Interview with John Vaninetti, *op. cit.*

LAND AS THE FUTURE

1. Figure based on total Bureau of Indian Affairs and other agency budgets of approximately $300 million per year divided by total number of Indians, 600,000.

2. Stan Steiner, *The New Indians*, pp. 133-34.

3. *Ibid.*, pp. 124-26.

4. Peter Paul Dorner, *The Economic Position of the American Indians: Their Resources and Potential for Development*, Doctoral Thesis, Harvard University, p. 175, February, 1959.

5. U.S. Senate Hearings, *Navajo Irrigation-San Juan-Chama Diversion*, pp. 103-04 in a statement by Howard W. Gorman, Member, Resources Committee of the Navajo Tribal Council, Window Rock, Arizona, as quoted in Dorner, *op. cit.*, p. 218.

6. *Hearings on the Department of the Interior and Related Agencies Appropriations for Fiscal Year 1969.* Interior Appropriations Subcommittee of the Senate Committee on Appropriations, 90 Cong. 2 sess., Part I, p. 430, February 23, 1968.

LAND AS A RESOURCE

1. Stewart Udall, *The Quiet Crisis*, p. 12.

2. "Paiute Indians Fight to Keep Lake," *The Christian Science Monitor*, May 27, 1968.

3. "Nevada Indians Fight for a Lake," *The New York Times*, February 25, 1969.

4. *Ibid.*

5. "Hickel Gets Caught in Oasis Row," *The Washington Post*, July 11, 1969.

LAND AS SACRED

1. Narrative of Black Elk, quoted in Jack D. Forbes, ed., *The Indian in America's Past*, p. 68.

2. *The Blue Lake Area: An Appeal from Taos Pueblo*, a pamphlet by the Taos Pueblo, p. 2.

3. Summary of Bureau of Indian Affairs position accompanying Statement by Stewart L. Udall, Secretary, Department of the Interior on S. 1624, S. 1625, and H.R. 3306. *Hearings before the Subcommittee on Indian Affairs of the Senate Committee on Interior and Insular Affairs*, 90 Cong., 2 sess.

3. Narrative of Black Elk, *loc. cit.*

LESSON I

1. Citizens Advocate Center interview, May 14, 1969.

2. Father Justus Writh, O.F.M., "Indian Men Need Jobs," Letter to the Editor, *The Gallup Independent*, June 19, 1968.

3. Federal Facilities for Indians, Tribal Relations with the Federal Government, Report by Mamie L. Mizen, Professional Staff

Member, Senate Appropriations Committee, 1965-66, Committee on Appropriations, p. 253.

4. Damon Lashbrook, "Forgotten Ones: Haskell Offers Indian Opportunity," *The University Daily Kansan*, December 10, 1968.

5. Carlos B. Embry, *America's Concentration Camps*, p. 33.

6. *People* v *Woody*, 40 Cal. Rptr. 69, 77-78, 394 P. 2d 819 (1964).

7. Letter from Stuart Trapp, Attorney-at-Law, to the Field Foundation, p. 3, January 22, 1969.

8. "The Indian: The Forgotten American," *Harvard Law Review*, Vol. 81, p. 1826, June 1968.

9. Citizens Advocate Center interview with Peter MacDonald, member of Navajo Tribal Council, April 1968.

10. Margaret Kuehlthau, "Loss of Scholarship Explodes Indian Girl's Dream of School," *Tucson Daily Citizen*, September 7, 1968.

11. Citizens Advocate Center interview, December 5, 1968.

12. Letter from Robert Leland, Attorney-at-Law, to Senator Howard W. Cannon, February 1965; Leland to Cannon, March 9, 1965; Leland to Cannon, May 18, 1965; Bureau of Indian Affairs News Release, March 5, 1966.

13. *Chemehuevi Newsletter*, March 1969.

LESSON II

1. Gary Orfield, "The Shuffling of the Papers," *A Study of the Termination Policy*, University of Chicago, Chapter 4, p. 4.

2. *Indian Resources Development Act of 1967*, Hearings before the House Subcommittee on Indian Affairs, Committee on Interior and Insular Affairs, 90 Cong. 1 sess., p. 48.

3. Memorandum from Secretary of the Interior Stewart L. Udall to the Chairman of the Department of the Interior Operating Criteria Committee, July 26, 1968.

4. Letter from Citizens' Advocate Center to Duard Barnes, Solicitor's Office—Indian Branch, Department of the Interior, July 24, 1968; Donald R. Marble, Circuit Rider Attorney, Montana Legal Services Association, North Central Montana Circuit Rider Attorney Office, to Haywood Burns, Staff Attorney, National Office of the Rights of the Indigent, May 14, 1968; Robert L. Bennett, Commissioner of Indian Affairs, to Donald R. Marble, February 25, 1969.

5. "White Man's Poverty Trap Holds Muckleshoot Indians in Misery," *Tacoma News Tribune*, May 5, 1968.

6. Letter from Martin Reiner, member of Indian Affairs Subcommittee, Syracuse Committee of Returned Volunteers, to Citizens' Advocate Center, February 27, 1969.

7. Statement by Mrs. Mildred Ballenger, Member, Chief's Executive Committee, Tahlequah, Oklahoma. *Hearings on the Education of Indian Children Before a Special Subcommittee on Indian Education of the Senate Committee on Labor and Public Welfare*, 90 Cong. 1 and 2 sess., Part II, p. 548, February 19, 1968.

8. Robert K. Thomas, "Powerless Politics," *New University Thought*, Vol. 4, p. 48, 1967.

9. *Ibid.*, p. 49.

10. William Bachrach, "An Assault in the Sixties," *The Humanist,* p. 183, September 1967.

11. E. E. Hagen and Louis C. Shaw, *The Sioux on the Reservations,* Center for International Studies, Massachusetts Institute of Technology, 1960, Chapter 6, p. 9., as quoted in William A. Brophy and Sophie D. Aberle, *The Indian: America's Unfinished Business,* p. 111.

LESSON III

1. Daniel Henninger and Nancy Esposito, "Regimented Non-Education: Indian Schools," *The New Republic,* p. 20, February 15, 1969.

2. Testimony at *Hearings on the Education of Indian Children before a Special Subcommittee on Indian Education of the Senate Committee on Labor and Public Welfare,* 90 Cong. 1 and 2 sess., Part I, pp. 35-36, December 14, 1967.

3. Statement by Harry W. Martin, Ph.D., Professor of Psychiatry (Sociology), University of Texas, at Indian Education Subcommittee Hearings, 90 Cong., 1 and 2 sess., Part V, p. 2163, October 1, 1968.

4. Official release of the testimony to be given by William Pensoneau, Vice President, National Indian Youth Council, at Indian Education Subcommittee Hearings, 90th Cong. 1 and 2 sess., February 24, 1969.

5. Ralph K. Andrist, *The Long Death,* p. 134.

6. "A Life of Disillusionment, Poverty—and Pride, Too: Indians Finally Get a Chance to Tell Their Own Story," *National Observer,* May 6, 1968.

7. Pensoneau, *op. cit.*

8. *Idem.*

9. *Idem.*

THE BARRIERS TO CHANGE

1. 25 U.S.C. § 2 (1968).

2. 25 U.S.C. § 48 (1968).

3. 25 U.S.C. § 452 (1968).

4. William A. Brophy and Sophie D. Aberle, *The Indian: America's Unfinished Business,* p. 75.

5. 25 U.S.C. § 175 (1968).

6. Indian Leaders Conference with Robert L. Bennett, Commissioner, Bureau of Indian Affairs, Spokane, Washington, p. 294, October 17-19, 1966.

7. Indian Leaders Conference with Robert L. Bennett, Commissioner, Bureau of Indian Affairs, Albuquerque, New Mexico, p. 1, November 21-22, 1966.

A CASE STUDY IN BUREAUCRACY

1. Alvin M. Josephy, Jr., *The American Indian and the Bureau of Indian Affairs—1969: A Study with Recommendations,* pp. 78-79, February 11, 1969.

2. *Ibid.*, p. 78.

3. Herbert E. Striner, "Towards a Fundamental Program for the Training, Employment and Economic Equality of the American Indian," p. 324, 1968.

4. Letter from Pyramid Lake Tribal Council to Secretary Udall, January 17, 1967.

5. Josephy, *op. cit.*, pp. 81-82.

6. Statement of the Quinault Tribe, Indian Leaders Conference with Robert L. Bennett, Commissioner, Bureau of Indian Affairs, Spokane, Washington, p. 231, October 17-19, 1966.

7. Stan Steiner, *The New Indians*, p. 256.

8. Report of the Community Development Committee, Albuquerque Area Tribal Leaders Conference with Robert L. Bennett, Commissioner, Bureau of Indian Affairs, Albuquerque, New Mexico, p. 9, November 21-23, 1966.

THE COMPROMISED ADVOCATE

1. "Position Paper: Indian Views on the Reorganization of the Bureau of Indian Affairs," National Congress of American Indians, Albuquerque, New Mexico, p. 2, May 6, 1969.

2. Alvin M. Josephy, Jr., *The American Indian and the Bureau of Indian Affairs—1969; A Study with Recommendations*, p. 15, February 11, 1969.

WINNING THE WEST: CONGRESS' UNFINISHED BUSINESS—Primary Footnotes

1. Stan Steiner, *The New Indians*, p. 243.

2. Ralph Nader, "Lo, The Poor Indian," *The New Republic*, p. 15, March 30, 1968.

3. Citizens' Advocate Center interview with Vine Deloria, Jr., October 3, 1968.

4. Report of the Senate Committee on Interior and Insular Affairs on the Nomination of Robert LaFollette Bennett of Alaska to be Commissioner of Indian Affairs, 89 Cong. 2 sess.

5. Citizens' Advocate Center interview, September, 1968.

CIVILIZING THE WHITE MAN

1. Lucy Kramer Cohen, ed., *The Legal Conscience: Selected Papers of Felix S. Cohen*, pp. 315-16.

2. Peter Farb, *Man's Rise to Civilization as Shown by the Indians of North America*, pp. 198-9.

3. *Ibid.*, pp. 123-4.

4. Jack D. Forbes, ed., *The Indian in America's Past*, pp. 65-66.

5. *Ibid.*, p. 65.

6. *Ibid.*, p. 66.

7. Cohen, *op. cit.*, p. 321.

8. Alvin M. Josephy, Jr., *The Indian Heritage of America*, pp. 34-45.

9. Irvin M. Peithmann, *Broken Peace Pipe*, p. 32, 1964.

10. Farb, *op. cit.*, p. 30.

11. Leonard W. Labaree, *et. al.* ed., *The Autobiography of Benjamin Franklin,* p. 199.

12. N. Scott Momaday, *House Made of Dawn,* p. 1.

13. Statements by Columbus Keahna, Don Wanatee, and Mrs. Patricia Brown, representatives of the Macquakie Tribe, Iowa, at *Hearings on the Education of Indian Children before a Special Subcommittee on Indian Education of the Senate Committee on Labor and Public Welfare,* 90 Cong. 1 and 2 sess., February 18, 1969.

14. Stan Steiner, *The New Indians,* p. 13.

15. David Martin Nez, "New Way, Old Way," quoted in Steiner, *op. cit.,* p. 131.

16. Chief Seattle, Duwamish Suquamish leader, speech to Governor Stevens' negotiating party at the Treaty of Point Elliott, 1885, reprinted in *An Uncommon Controversy,* prepared for The American Friends Service Committee, p. 29, 1967.

17. Chief Black Hawk of the Sac and Fox tribes, upon surrendering to the U.S. in 1832, quoted in Farb, *op. cit.,* p. 292.

18. Janet McCloud, University of Washington Law School, Law Day Ceremonies, May 1, 1969.

19. Adrienne Koch and William Peden, ed., *The Life and Selected Writings of Thomas Jefferson,* p. 221, 1944.

20. Farb, *op. cit.,* pp. 45-56.

21. Felix Cohen, "Indian Rights and the Federal Courts," Minnesota Law Review. Vol. 24, pp. 145, 156.

22. Farb, *op. cit.,* p. 43.

23. Albert Wahrhaftig, "The Folk Society as Type," Wayne State University, pp. 9-11, June, 1968.